T0099868

─Will the Real──────
WORLD
Please Stand up?

A guide to everyday spirituality

JOHN STEGMAIER

BALBOA.
PRESS

A DIVISION OF HAY HOUSE

Copyright © 2012 by John Steigmaier.

All rights reserved. No part of this book may be used or reproduced by any means, graphic, electronic, or mechanical, including photocopying, recording, taping or by any information storage retrieval system without the written permission of the publisher except in the case of brief quotations embodied in critical articles and reviews.

ISBN: 978-1-4525-5004-6 (sc)
ISBN: 978-1-4525-5052-7 (e)
ISBN: 978-1-4525-5003-9 (hc)

Library of Congress Control Number: 2012906366

Balboa Press books may be ordered through booksellers or by contacting:

Balboa Press
A Division of Hay House
1663 Liberty Drive
Bloomington, IN 47403
www.balboapress.com
1-(877) 407-4847

Because of the dynamic nature of the Internet, any web addresses or links contained in this book may have changed since publication and may no longer be valid. The views expressed in this work are solely those of the author and do not necessarily reflect the views of the publisher, and the publisher hereby disclaims any responsibility for them.

The author of this book does not dispense medical advice or prescribe the use of any technique as a form of treatment for physical, emotional, or medical problems without the advice of a physician, either directly or indirectly. The intent of the author is only to offer information of a general nature to help you in your quest for emotional and spiritual well-being. In the event you use any of the information in this book for yourself, which is your constitutional right, the author and the publisher assume no responsibility for your actions.

Any people depicted in stock imagery provided by Thinkstock are models, and such images are being used for illustrative purposes only.
Certain stock imagery © Thinkstock.

Printed in the United States of America

Balboa Press rev. date: 04/24/12

Will the Real World Please Stand Up?

The paradox of our Time

We've learned how to make a living, but not a life. We've added years to life not life to years. We've been all the way to the moon and back, but have trouble crossing the street to meet a new neighbor. We conquered outer space but not inner space. We've done larger things, but not better things.
Dr. Bob Moorehead

At the center of your being you have the answer; you know who you are and you know what you want.
Lao Tzu

Dear "Real" world,
Today I ask that you see me for who I am. I am not my body. I am not my mind. I am infinite being, and we are the same. Be blessed in this understanding and may we all move forward in our spiritual evolution, as one family.

Love

John

For Daniel: You were my role model
For Mom: You were my discipline
For Dad: You were my belief
For Angie: You were my inspiration

Table of Contents

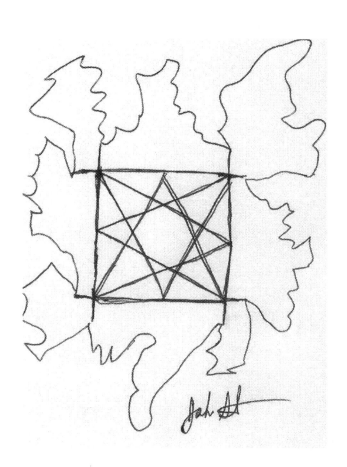

Section 1:
Introduction and Foundation.

1. This first section, you are exposed to the events, thoughts, responses, etc that have occurred in my life and in the world that have shaped my thought process.
2. Additionally, you will note that an extensive amount of quotes, written or spoken by highly enlightened people are cited to support various ideas in the book. Those not cited are simply ideas that I wished to emphasize.
3. Finally, I have left some blank pages at the end of this book. If you are like me, I always need a place to make notes on particular ideas that strike a chord with me.

Reader's Orientation

This book has been written in several parts. The first, delineating what I have felt for a great many years, and what I think many of us feel, about the existence of two separate worlds. I call them the <u>Spirit "real" World</u> and the <u>Ego "real" World</u>... these are perspectives and are just as "real" to the people that view life in one way or the other.

Secondly, there are a number of societal comparisons from the perspective of each of these worlds, based on observations, perspectives and weaving in the philosophies of several amazing life teachers.

This book is concluded with a discussion of the choices that we must all make over the course of our lives based on which world we "see." There is no right and wrong dualism here.

Additionally there are "turning points" between those who live a spiritual existence and those that live in ego world. Those reading a spiritual book may seek practical methods to move from one perspective to another. These are concepts, which tie these together and help the journey of our life, as we see it, be founded in a manner in which we are more at ease.

To many these two "worlds" seem paradoxical, but, as you will see, these worlds can be interwoven and are deeply connected.

Throughout this book, there are quotes from a great many spiritual leaders past and present to support the thoughts, and correlations drawn. All of the quotes that I use from other people are cited so that you may seek out more valuable information from those that strike a particular chord of resonance with you.

A Life of Lessons

As most people have, I have dealt with peaks and valleys in life and have sometimes chosen the path of least resistance. Other times life seemed to hit me "up-side the head" like a two by four, and THEN headed down another path. What I can unequivocally say is that EVERYTHING that has taken place and led me to this point has been an important lesson and has pointed me in the direction I am moving. This may have occurred intentionally by learning from great spiritual teachers or by participating in accidental life lessons.

One truth that seems inarguable is that the most difficult times in my life have also been the times that have lead me to my greatest discoveries. I think that is true for most people. I have learned that when times seem difficult, I keep moving forward.

"Never Give in; Never, Never, Never, Never."
Winston Churchill

That does not mean that I fought the situation.... On the contrary, I am vigilant in locating the lesson to be learned and in which I will evolve.

We often look at the most troublesome, difficult times from the perspective of the martyr. If we can start to see that these are the most important times in our lives, we will begin to turn life into a wonderful, exciting journey, rather than a burden.

*"If you are facing the right direction, all
you need to do is keep walking."*
Buddhist Proverb

It is my hope that this book triggers something in your mind that stimulates you to ask: "Am I facing the right direction?"

I am no monk that has meditated on the meaning of life throughout the course of my existence, although I do regularly meditate, while having nothing but pure thoughts and a clean mind. I am not a learned scholar of Cambridge, although I have read and studied great works by very intelligent people for the last twenty years. I am a man with a humble background, one that may seem familiar to many of you, which is why I feel it is important to get these thoughts on to paper.

I teach high school chemistry, physics, and biology, but I know that science does not have all of the answers. I try to always teach my students to constantly discover and question. I believe that they should never accept things that are observed at face value.

I start every school year by saying to my students:

There is NO such thing as a scientific fact!"

There are theories and laws, but for something to be a fact, means that there can be no other explanation. I have studied enough science to know that we don't know as much as we think we do. Only our egos, even in science, legitimize such a concept of absolute fact.

*There is a world of discovery and mystery to be uncovered, and
new ideas to be conceived for those who think outside of the box.*

Foundation: The Life That Shaped The Thoughts

MY TEACHING EXPERIENCE SPANS over twenty years and seven different high schools in six different cities and three different states. These schools were in impoverished areas, relatively affluent areas and everything in between. Some were schools with students that had major behavioral issues. There were other schools where students were rarely in administrative straits. I only share this to express to you one observation that I believe:

> *When you arrive at the heart of a person, I mean the true core of a human heart, after the fears have been uncovered and loved away, that people basically want to go down a path of enlightenment and higher connectivity to their source.*

I have lived my life with this belief for many years. Some people call that naïve; perhaps it is, but I can tell you that this has been a happier and more joyful perspective than at times when my perspective was careful and guarded.

Raised the youngest of nine children in a devoutly Catholic family there was seldom time for contemplation. Being born in the early 1960's had an interesting influence on me.

I was not really old enough to know who John F. Kennedy was, but I certainly was affected by the impact of his death, and how devastating a single death can be.

I wasn't really a hippy but was heavily influenced by the desire for a nation to express peace and love as I grew up in the 1960s. This was a real energy.

> *They possess a core belief set revolving around*
> *the values of peace and love as being essential*
> *in an increasingly globalized society...*
> Urban Dictionary definition of hippy

I remember great importance placed on racial equity spearheaded by the great Dr. Martin Luther King. The immense loss of the enlightened Reverends life brought, to the forefront, the importance of viewing all humans as one people instead of separate... indeed all life as a part of the same loving energy.

I grew up in the 1960s and 1970s knowing that the world was all about peace and love.

> *In the 1950s Maslow (Abraham Maslow 1908-1970) believed*
> *that only 2% of the population had achieved self-actualization*
> *(Maslow's hierarchy of needs). The mid-1960s changed all*
> *that when masses of people began to search for the higher*
> *values, such as unconditional love and spiritual wisdom*
> Owen Waters
> *The Shift: The Revolution in Human Consciousness*

As my beliefs developed, I cultivated a great sense of humanity as well as environmental consciousness. None of this seemed out of the ordinary, or noble...just status quo.

In my little town of Woodstock Illinois, at the age of ten, I thought everyone wanted the best for each other and peace throughout the land. It was right about that time when the newspapers were filled with the scandal of Watergate. This was my first real taste of the fear side of people... the ego.

In the late seventies, I moved with my parents to Tucson, Arizona and attended high school as well as participated in sports. I was large and in charge, and quite hormonal (sound familiar?), but basically a good kid.

There were three or four teachers there that had a profound effect on my life. The care and concern for me as I strayed from the straight and narrow path by one teacher in particular stands out. His name was Jack Combs. He was the primary reason that I pursued a teaching career...Thanks Jack!

I attended College at Northern Arizona University, and learned a great many lessons. There were also *significant* turning points in my life during this time. I struggled with grades and focus early in my college career, but eventually it all came full circle and I received my degree. A significant life teacher as well as Chemistry professor was Dr. Scott Savage. It was a difficult, and trying time. He challenged me and inspired me as he had done for many thousands of students. Thank you Scott!

I student taught at Coconino High school in Flagstaff. That was when I met the third of the truly inspirational education teachers in my life: Dr. Jim David. Jim was my mentor while I student taught. At that time he had been teaching for 27 years and still did it because he loved the kids. He was not sour and was an inspiration to me. He had great patience and he taught me that every person has something special about them, and they want you to know what it is (by the way Jim, I am still doing the Christmas project)... thanks Jim!

I went from student teaching in Flagstaff to teaching In Gunnison Colorado with one-year stops in Lake Havasu and Oak Creek Arizona. I stayed in Gunnison for seven years and coached as well. I still do both because I love both. I do not mean to minimize these experiences here, of which there were many. I will be sharing many of these through out this book.

In 1995 my mom had a stroke. This led me to move back to Tucson, Arizona in order to help out my parents. My mother passed away or crossed over, in 2001 and I moved into my fathers' house while acting as his caregiver at night until 2008 when I moved to Idaho. My father has always been my hero. There is great joy in recalling in the time that I had with both mom and dad. They taught me the greatest lesson of life:

That everyone deserves unconditional love

In a way, they were the first hippies in my life. Thank you Mom and Dad!

While living back in Tucson, I taught for eight years at Marana high school; a neat farming community that was very accepting and hard working. In 2008 I moved to Boise, Idaho to live and teach.

I adore the kids that I work with as well as all of the students that have shaped my life over the years, and still love what I do for a living. I can honestly say that my students teach me more lessons than I could ever hope to teach them.

My spiritual journey has taken great form in learning from spiritual teachers. Teachers such as Wayne Dyer, Thomas Moore, Gerald Jampolski, Robert Fulghum, Eckhart Tolle, Deepak Chopra, Michael Bernard Beckwith, have taught me many lessons; not the least of which is to always look for the good…it is there. I have also received counseling from great spiritual people, whether or not they meant to. All of which have helped me to become more self-aware, and live my life by creativity and love.

The passing of my eldest brother preceded the passing of my mother. He was someone that enriched everyone's life that met him. This all seemed to take place very close to each other and I, along with my family, struggled to make any sense out of it, and to find the good. It was a genuinely painful time, but I learned about caring for others and how much people can give at a difficult time (more evidence that all people are somehow connected to a loving source).

The following are some stories about significant spiritual moments in my life.

One occurred exactly one month after Dan passed. I experienced an amazingly real dream with Dan in it. In it he was going over some financial things with me (he was a financial consultant and banker while in this physical life), then he told me he had to go, so he left the room and walked to two sets of stairs; one heading up and one heading down. He started up but then came back into the room to give me a hug. The dream ended at that moment. When I awoke I was so happy and so certain that he had actually come to see me. It was also the first significant awakening in my life. The second story is about my moms passing.

Mom was struggling in ICU. Every breath she took was a miniature battle to make her lungs expand and contract and the nurse was alerted to her diminishing readings on the monitor. All the other family members had gone home to rest. I was the only one in the hospital room when the nurse told me to get everyone back to the hospital right away. I went outside to use my cell phone. Of course it was a grey afternoon and it had begun to drizzle. I tried to get through to dad and my sister, but it was as if all my attempts were being blocked. After fifteen minutes or so I went back in, unable to reach anyone and as I walked in the room, the nurse told me she had passed. As I keeled over in gut-wrenching stomach pain, the nurse said that many people, when they are this close, hold on until their loved-ones are out of the room, then simply let go. It was inconceivable at this time, to think that my mom was gone and that she had the love in her heart and the will to wait until I had left the room so that I would not have to experience her passing. What an amazing spirit!

This was the second significant awakening moment in my life. In the time it took for the rest of the family to arrive at the hospital, I looked at my mom's life capsule. I realized that she was not there. She was all around me. Through my pain and deep sadness, I had a sense of her being free and at peace. I knew then and I know now that she is part of the collective energy that I call Gods Loving Universe. I love you mom.

Perhaps the largest of my life influences was my father. My dad is my inspiration. What an amazing man! He grew up a farmer in Minnesota, went to Loyola Dental School and was a dentist for fifty-four years, including in the US Navy during World War II. The father of nine kids, he, along with mom, taught us a strong sense of love. Two of my lasting images are of him always working hard; sometimes at the office, but other times busting his butt working on the farm we lived at.

The other memory I will always have are his hugs. He even hugged his patients. He gave me the gift of strong self-belief and love. I look up to him as a hero. Born in 1919, he recently passed over to the spiritual realm at the age of ninety-two. To the day that he passed he was a loving, caring man that was active in church, socially, and to this day, I believe he could repair anything that is broken…including hearts. I love you dad.

Now I don't go through this other than for you to hopefully gain an understanding of the people and some of the turning points that have molded my mind, body, and spirit. We all are who we are due to the influences that we accept in our life and the way that we perceive and respond to.

Section 2:
Perspectives

This section delves into various perspectives of the concepts involved in Ego "Real" World and Spirit "real" World.
In addition to the various perspectives of the "real" world, there is discussion on various turning points in life, the Sanskrit concepts of Namaste', The Law of Attraction, and a fair amount of scientific background regarding the idea of spirituality, energy, and our universe.

Turning Points

A man is but the product of his thoughts.
What he thinks, he becomes
Mahatma Gandhi

ISN'T IT INTERESTING THE way in which some people respond to the things they attract into their life in various manners? As children, we are "taught" cognitive lessons which shift our perspective from a place of feeling to a place of thinking. This adds to the separation from others that began as our bodies entered the physical world. As we continue to grow, we are taught to use our minds and physical skills more and more and to disregard much of the "feeling" places of our lives. As events unfold in our lives, we view them with what we have "learned" previously and it changes the way that we see things from that point on. So everything that occurs and how we interpret it affects the way that we interpret everything else.

Imagine what would happen if you could go back and rethink the way that you looked at things long ago. It would have a domino effect on the away that you have seen everything since then. Say for example that when you were nine years old, there was a gun accident at your house. As a nine year old, you would process that differently than you would as a forty year old. But the way that this incident made you feel would have an effect on the way that you felt about guns the rest of your life. Perhaps it keeps you away from guns the rest of your life. In turn this keeps you from joining the police force. If you went back and changed the way that this incident made you feel, it would change how you felt about a great many other events that followed in which a gun may have been involved. This would have a significant change in your life. This is one example of a possible turning point. These occur every day and they can all change the direction in which we point our lives. The key is to already have an idea of the direction that you wish to move. That way when these turning points occur, they don't have such a great effect on your journey.

In each of our lives there are a great many *turning points* that have occurred; points where you could turn left, right, or move straight. The choice that you made contributed to who you are and how you look at life. This concept is clearly illustrated in a series of well-made movies called "Back to the Future". Several times Doc Brown (played by Christopher Lloyd) cautions Marty McFly (played by Michael J. Fox) about tampering with the course of history and how the things we do can affect the direction of life.

I hope that this book helps people recognize and learn different perspectives, if for no other reason, than to develop the ability to empathize. I hope that many will see that some of these major turning points actually may be re-evaluated and perhaps there is a realization that we can change the way that we reacted to our turning points. What if you could rethink concepts that you learned as a small child or only last year or maybe in another life, and then reframe the events of your life with your new way of thinking? That certainly would have an impact on where you are in life and where you expect to go. This concept extends to everyone around you as well.

Remember that the way that you interact with
others has an effect on them as well as you, all based
on theirs and your previous turning points.

Here is a simple example of what I am trying to illustrate: As a teacher I come in contact with all types of students in high school who are all busily going through various phases in order to find that niche in life that is uniquely theirs. Early in my teaching career, I came in contact with students that wore all black, including their finger nails and hair, had pins stuck into various places in their body, upside-down crosses carved, yes... carved, into their arms, and had propensities toward, violence directed at themselves and others. Additionally, they portrayed a distinctive dark, depression. Using a societal word, they were classified as "Goths." As years went along, the style took hold with all types of students, and I ended up with many students taking on this look; even in my honors chemistry classes. Upon gazing at them on the first day of class, my initial response was, "What is a kid like this doing in my honors Chemistry?" I would respond to them with a certain degree of guarded fear and apprehension. You can imagine what this response probably did to the way that they interacted back. We had developed a relationship built on fear and negativity. I would venture to say that many people might respond to young adults with this style in the same manner. We often judge everyone we see based on their outward appearance rather than looking at the spirit and trying to make a connection.

After a period of time, the spirit in me began to get my attention, and I realized that this student was not the evil, sociopath that I had made them to be in my mind. When I started to respond to ALL of my students in love and kindness, I learned so much more about myself than I ever knew, and we were able to enlighten each other. That same student that I was reluctant to open myself to earlier became one of my favorite students and teachers after bearing my spirit to them.

Namaste'

I honor the place in you where the entire Universe resides.
I honor the place of love, of light, of truth, of peace.
I honor the place within you where if
you are in that place in you,
And I am in that place in me, there is only one of us"
Ram Dass
Spiritual teacher
Author: Be Here Now

THINK ABOUT THE PEOPLE that we come in contact with every day, and how many judgments we make about them based on past *turning points*. Now think about how that framework had colored the way that you treat others from work, at home, school, and just in public.

Isn't it interesting how so many people are not willing to even make eye contact with others in public because they are afraid of being judged or of judging the other in a negative manner.

Let me challenge you, now to the first *turning point* of this book: Go out today in public… the coffee shop, grocery store, ball park, and look people square in the eye and smile and say 'hi." You will be amazed at the response from them. You will also be amazed at how it will change your perspective. Some people will shy away or even question your intention. But if you smile with sincerity, the response will warm you down to your toes.

The Hindu word Namaste' means, literally, the God in me greats the God in you. Instead of avoiding others, great them with the knowing of a brother or sister, and you will see the change in you both.

If you don't think that you have any effect, think about the number of people that you come in contact with on a daily basis. I believe that everyone we meet has an effect on us and we on him or her. That's a lot of effect. In what way do you affect the people in your life? Do you make them glad that they met you and help them feel happy to be alive?

If you will accept this turning point into your life, I can assure you that you will never want to return to the recluse, surly ways that many people travel through on a daily basis.

Arlo Guthrie sang a song called Alice's Restaurant back in the 1960s. To say the least, it was a satirical folk song aimed at ending the Viet Nam war. He implored people all over to sing a chorus of Alice's Restaurant as a means to end war. Arlo called it the Alice's restaurant anti-massacre movement.

Well folks, if we can all start to look each other in the eye and greet each other, we may start a movement that will do more than end war. We may all begin to recognize the God in each other. What a powerful way to think of another person.

Namaste' says it all: The God in me greets the God in you. The spirit in me meets the same spirit in you. We all know that there is a spirit in us. Deep inside we have an understanding that there is an ethereal entity that actually is observing and our body is simply a housing unit for a short biological lifetime.

In the movie, What the Bleep Do We Know, this inner driving force was called the observer. Wayne Dyer calls it his Senior Partner. In quiet, alone moments, we are aware of this presence. The spirit is in you and in everyone... Namaste'

What is the "real" world?

"Remember this dear friend.
Right now in this moment, you are either
listening to the voice of God or you are needlessly
enmeshed in your own psychodrama"
Paul Ferrini
Love Without Conditions
Reflections of the Christ Mind

WHEN I WAS GROWING up there was a television game show program called <u>To Tell the Truth</u>. This game show brought on three anonymous people who all claimed to be the same person, and it was up to a panel of guest celebrities to ask poignant questions in order to determine who the "real" person actually was. At the end of the program and after all of the guest celebrities had made their guesses, the host would ask, "Will the real (insert name here) please stand up?" This was an intriguing program, which I suppose is why it seemed to have such a long run. Five versions of this program ran over forty years. I am using the analogy of this program to name this book and in doing so, make an attempt in identifying the 'Real" world.

I am using this analogy because I think that introspective people ask questions during the entirety of their life in a quest to determine what the "real" world is and hopefully to learn the necessary lessons through introspection, and listening to the spirit in order to make themselves whole and complete members of this world. We seem to be on a constant quest to find out who the "real" me is.

I feel that many people see themselves at the end of their body-temple life, at the end of the game show, asking the question: Will the real world please stand up? This we do in an effort to reassure ourselves that we have made the right choices and learned the appropriate lessons during our mortal life. I have found more often than not that people who have lived a long time develop or at least recognize their ability to see the world in the spiritual sense... That is, they have used these questions and looked deep enough inside to see passed the veil of the false self of ego, fear, guilt, opposition and duality.

Instead they see the truth that we are all amazing, beautiful spiritual beings. I believe that we know this as infants but lack the correlative skills to express this, then as we develop language skills and are encouraged to think, our egos and fears enter the equation as we are taught to enter this contentious world where we see everyone as separate rather than all part of the source. As my father aged he was very lucid and I really believe that he saw people in the spiritual sense. That was why he loved everyone.

I saw God in his eyes... it looked like...LOVE.

The Ego World and the Spiritual World

*"Two people have been living in you all of your life. One
is the ego, garrulous, demanding, hysterical, calculating;
the other is the hidden spiritual being whose still voice of
wisdom you have only rarely heard or attended to."*
Sogyal Rinpoche, Tibetan teacher
Author of the Tibetan Book of Living and Dying

WHAT IS THE REAL world? One day, my friend, who is a social
studies teacher, and I had a long discussion about why I don't watch
the news or read the newspaper. As a social studies teacher, this was
his "real" world, and part of his job as well.

I began to think about what that meant. So many things have
occurred in my life since then, that I think I may have a different
idea about what that means than most others.

To many, the "real" world is only what they can experience by
tasting, touching, smelling, hearing, or seeing. In short the "real"
world is contained within the physical existence that we learned
about in science class. It is the cerebral, cognitive world that we
ingest, process, and then reciprocate outwardly.

Few people put much credibility into aspects of life that cannot
be detected using conventional methods. Further, isn't it possible to
"feel" love or anger or other emotions? How can a hug affect us in
a way such as to make a person "feel" better? Is that real? I believe
that enlightened people are simply those that choose to see the

world in a spiritual sense. They see love and God where others may see competition and "badness."

After caring for my father and focusing more on peoples energy, I believe that most elderly people have been removed from the physical world far enough so as to reevaluate their perspective. Many become enlighten as a result.

As a chemistry teacher, I understand that our model of the atom leaves a great deal of room for extrapolation. Do we truly understand the "real" world? Are we separate entities from it or does it run through us, thus connecting us all?

Additionally, quantum physics can turn all of our solid five senses into something that resembles more like a fairy-tale. More and more research in the quantum world has lead scientists to believe that ALL things are actually comprised of energy with interacting forces that give us the sense of matter, rather than the reality of it. By this thought process, there is no difference between you and I or a tree or a rock…It is all energy, that vibrates at various frequencies. I will comment more on this later.

Many people see the real world as what is portrayed in the news or in the newspaper. The news, like any other business is attempting to gain your attention.

I have always been amazed that dualistic thinking people tend to believe and become more interested in negative than positive information. I observe people completely absorbed by every negative, hateful word that comes from newscasts, and when they walk away from the television, they feel better informed… more intelligent. When a group of Muslim religious zealots attacked the United States on September 11, 2001, every station on the television was completely possessed by the spectacle of the towers being struck by a large airliner and each tower crumbling. This went beyond the need to report the incident. I watched it for one hour and the image of the attack was shown no less than ten times in that hour.

It burned an indelible mark in the minds of those that continued to watch and absorb this over and over.

People, in general, don't realize that they have been exposed to a toxin. This toxin is subtle and eats away at the truth; that we are spiritual beings undergoing a temporary human existence for the purpose of recognizing and sharing our gifts.

When was the last headline you read about someone who saved a child from a burning building? Oh, once in a while these stories come across the television, but most people tend to see them as "feel good" stories and await the "real" news. Let's face it. Negativity sells!

Try this experiment with a group of acquaintances to illustrate this point: The next time that you are scheduled to meet a small group of people, when you arrive, tell them a story about an unbelievable accident that you just witnessed while on your way to meet them. You can embellish it and add incredible plot lines with police helicopters and the National Guard. Notice how many people accept the story and, indeed are completely engrossed. Don't let this go on too long before you come clean and tell everyone that this did not really happen. This has always fascinated me.

The antithesis of this experiment would be to arrive and tell everyone that you just witnessed the most amazing act of heroism or kindness. Many people might respond in an incredulous or apathetic manner...why? Why do so many people have difficulty believing that this world is filled with others performing positive, life-affirming acts. It is you know. There is so much beauty in this world, yet we as a society tend to fix our gaze on negatives. Often we are aghast at such acts, but are incapable of looking away... not terribly life-affirming.

You don't have to look far for other examples of this. Most web-browsers have news headlines. Read them with a speculative mind about what kind of headline they are. Do they make you feel better or worse after you read them? You will see that the news which is low energy, bringing your emotions to a lower level outweigh uplifting news by an excruciating amount. It would not be there, if it did not sell folks. That is the nature of capitalism.

Is this dualistic, good versus bad existence "real?" Sounds like an absurd question to many, doesn't it? Let's compare two kinds of "real" worlds. They are both just as real and just as significant to those people who choose to live in them.

I have extrapolated much of his meaning from Great authors like Wayne Dyer, Eckhart Tolle, Michael Bernard Beckwith, Paul Ferrini, Thomas Moore and many others. All of these amazing spiritual leaders are listed at the end of this book. I would encourage any person looking for spiritual guidance and a means to make sense of it all to read these books.

The Ego "real" World

"See your choice of victimhood and be willing to release it."
Paul Ferrini
Love Without Conditions

THE EGO WORLD CORRELATES to what many call the physical world. It is the world that sees all matter as separate, including us. As such, this world leads us to compete and bring others down in order to raise ourselves. It is the world of scarcity and dualistic thinking. This is the real world that is contentious, confrontational, competitive, a world in which we can only get ahead at the expense of another. This is typified by the saying that I saw on a bumper sticker over twenty years ago:

He who dies with the most toys, wins

This is the ultimate in separation and competition among each other. This is the ultimate in ego.

The Ego world is a world in which a person sees them
self as separate from everyone else and God
Wayne Dyer

This concept is taken to the highest level in a concept known as solipsism. This philosophical concept is self defined as the idea that only ones own mind exists and nothing else.

This is a world that judges others and each person feels judged, often by their appearances, how much money that they make, the possessions they display, the job they have, or status in life. This is the world where divorces turn nasty so that each person gets "their share." This is the world where fights start because someone looks at someone else in an offensive manner. This is the world of war, and winners and losers. This life sees the "real" world as that which is seen on the news and in the papers. A covert issue with this is that you do not have control over what you are exposed to.

> *If you trust your television, what you get is what you got.*
> *When they own the information, they can bend it all they want*
> *John Mayer*
> *Waiting on the World to Change*

This ego world is ruled by fear! The vast majority of products sold on TV advertising utilize some form of fear to motivate their buyers, from insurance to bottled water. This fear leads to hostile takeovers in the business world, cheating in the sports world, and even road-rage in the driving world. This fear leads people to purchase alarm systems for their homes, cars, and stores.

> *It has raised the level of fear among people about every*
> *aspect of their lives, in such a way as to imprison our*
> *bodies, and minds, and shield us from our spirits.*

While we may feel that we gain security, we lose a fair amount of life's greatest pleasures here. People feel safer while "locked" in their house, with the top-of-the line security system. They are afraid to open up to their neighbors, to open their homes as well as their hearts to those in need.

Trust is all but nonexistent. Those that choose this view would never think about leaving their homes unlocked or their car, unprotected for five minutes without engaging the alarm.

Part of our kid's development should be the socialization, yet they are protected and shielded in their homes while attaching to their computers, instead of playing in the park. Patriots claim freedom in this country but this sounds a bit like incarceration... not freedom.

Children have to play inside so they don't disappear
Train
Calling All Angels

Ego-centered, separatist fear has led a nation into a constant state of alarm concerning national security. 9-11 has taken on a whole new meaning in the last several years. It has changed our perspective on world politics, and the word "Terrorism" has allowed government officials to infringe on peoples freedoms and act in ways that are uncharacteristic all in the name of patriotism. Anyone not in compliance with many of these fear-based tactics is labeled as un-American or a terrorist-sympathizer by the same institutions that are designed to protect human rights. This type of ego driven policy has been in effect for many generations. Years ago it was the Communists, now it is terrorists. As long as we see "bad" guys, the ego will seek new ways to build greater walls.

In dualistic, egoic thinking there is never enough to go around. Scarcity is the manner in which these people go about their lives. There is never enough so they have to out-compete someone for their piece of the pie and that means that someone else loses out on a piece. That is scarcity thinking.

An ego-based approach to life is superficial, and external. It is DRIVEN by fear; fear of attack, fear of loss, and even fear of self. All of these fears are based on us being separate.

Think about it. If we all felt like we were part of one common source fear and loss could not exist... how can you take from yourself?

This approach to life fills us with status symbols like our achievements, our possessions, and our appearances. The ego world sees the attainment of such items as success.

Unfortunately this approach leaves us empty inside...if we take the time to look. Ego based existence is combative and sees the world as competitive. Because of this approach, each ego-centered person spends a good deal of his or her lives being offended by something or someone. In some cases people are even offended by God! They will go to all sorts of lengths to get even with the offender. You see it on roads and in stores... everywhere you look.

> *Self importance is mans greatest enemy.*
> *It requires that one spend most of ones life*
> *offended by something or someone*
> *Carlos Castaneda*
> *Anthropologist and author*

Think about the last time that you felt offended by a driver cutting you off in traffic, or someone else edging in the front of the line at a bank or coffee shop. Ego-centered individuals are offended so easily. It is far more difficult to be at peace with this and wish this person forgiveness and love. In this type of world, we can only win by hurting others, or depleting their existence because there is only a limited amount of "stuff." The only way that we can get ours is by taking someone else's.

To people that utilize an ego-based focus; there is no such thing as abundance. In order to win, someone else must lose. Those that live an ego-based life are motivated by what is in it for them.

A person can even look like they are helping others, but the motivation is far from altruistic. A great many people will publicly announce their magnanimous philanthropy in papers or to others around them for recognition of how caring they are. Martyrdom can be the ultimate in this type of ego-centrism.

Instead of someone else losing, it is the Martyr that loses so that others may gain. This seemingly altruistic act, is often motivated by recognition for their act. That is just another form of status.

To the people that live their lives from this perspective, there is no connection between all of the people in this world, the trees, animals, and all other entities. This existence necessitates that all gains come from the depletion of another or us.

In this book I am referring to this perspective as the Ego "real" World. Here are two definitions of ego.

1. *An inflated feeling of pride in your superiority to others.*
2. *Self: your consciousness of your own identity.*
    wordnet.princeton.edu

I am not suggesting that everyone who fits into what I call the Ego "real" World has an inflated feeling of pride in superiority, but there certainly is a fair amount of that.

Allow me to add an addendum to the second definition in order to fit my definition of the Ego "real" World:

> *Your consciousness of your own identity, as separate from everyone else, and from God… thank you Dr. Dyer.*

The Spirit "real" World

Every time that you heal a judgmental thought or feeling of
separation, It is felt by every mind and heart in the universe
Paul Firrini
Love Without Conditions

Let me preface this by stating that my discussion of this world
is not based solely on the world beyond tangibility.

This world is primarily based on the concept of all
entities originating from the same source and being
constantly in connection with each other.

We all crave it deep down, but it is masked by ego.

I just want something to hold on to and
a little of that human touch
Bruce Springsteen
Human Touch

Have you ever held another persons hand… I mean genuinely
held it? Have you felt the energy that has joined yours? Isn't that as
real as electricity, or sunlight, or heat?

It amazes me at how many people see themselves in the ego
world yet acknowledge the existence of a spirit world. Perhaps they
are a little afraid to fully delve into the possibilities of this world

concerned that they may see things in their spirit that they would rather not look at or be confronted by.

Unlike the ego-based existence, the spirit-based existence is one centered around love. In a spiritual based approach to life we focus on virtues like love, friendship, inner strength, belief, faith, service to others, spirituality, connectedness to all creation. All of these characteristics support the idea of existence being one instead of separate entities. Each of these God-acts is supportive of all life.

To an ego-based life these things may seem weak and soft, but it actually requires a greater and different type of strength and enlightenment to partake in these high-energy spiritual avenues, rather than the low-energy fear or anger.

> *The spirit-based existence understands that*
> *God is Love. What can be stronger than God?*
> *Therefore, what can be stronger than love?*

These are the strongest most powerful feelings and drives in the universe. This existence requires us to accept the idea that we are all connected. We must see that all existence has the same common ground. There is no judgment. There is only love. Other, low energy thoughts are developed in the ego world, and are creations of fear and feeling of separation. They do not come from source.

In the Spirit "real" World, what is good for you is good for me. Creation is the foundation of growth and advancement instead of competition. Together we can create anything our minds can conceive and our hearts can dream. I do not need to lose in order for you to win. We both succeed by helping each other attract the abundance of the universe.

In abundance, spiritual thinking, there is always more. We live in an abundant universe. The most important thing that an abundance-thinking person does is helping others achieve their success. This keeps the flow of abundance moving along. To those living in this life, the universe is friendly and joyful and we are all a part of the same common source, so in helping others, they help the entire universe.

The term Universe comes from the Latin word *universum*, which means, all literally turned into one. What a marvelous way to think about the loving, kind, generous universe in which we all participate.

Spirit-based life sees only beauty in life...not in the manner that ego-life defines beauty. This is not a beauty defined by hair color, facial features, body morphology, and weight or body composition. This is the deep beauty that moves us down to our soul from a sunset, a particularly moving piece of music, an act of kindness that is given or received, or the tenderness of a parent with their newly born child. This beauty touches your soul, and everyone is capable of experiencing it.

> *Beauty is not pleasantness of form, but rather quality*
> *that invites absorption and contemplation*
> Thomas Moore
> *Care of the Soul*

When was the last time that you contemplated beauty? Have you ever felt beauty so deep that you could feel tears well up in your eyes? This beauty is in all things, all living organisms, and all inanimate objects. It is in the feelings that we have, and the energy that we share.

All too often we deprive ourselves of this beauty, dismissing it as unnecessary or unreal. In all situations, you have the ability to see the beauty of another and yourself. All you need to do is choose to contemplate it and absorb it. Creation can only be beautiful. Do you see it?

This applied, heart-based perspective, I will be referring to, mostly, as the Spirit "real" World during the course of this book.

The term Spirit comes from the Latin, spiritus, which is derived from the term spirare. This means to breathe. Since we must breathe to live, perhaps this is an indication as to which is truly the "real" world.

Which existence do you choose to live in? It's your choice.

You attract what you think about... whether you fear it or love it

When you change the way that you look at
things, the things that you look at change
Wayne Dyer
Power of Intention

THE GREAT LAW OF attraction is simple: You attract what you think about. There is more to it of course. There is also a level of feeling and attachment to these things, which also plays a role.

In every situation, you can choose an ego thought like fear, or anger, or you can choose a spirit thought, like love and compassion. The manifestation may be unconscious, but something WILL arrive. One of the keys is to see yourself as the observer of yourself, so that you can make the choice between a separatist me-you approach, or a feeling of togetherness and service.

Those who fear or hate something may not want that situation in their life but the shear intensity of their thoughts and emotions will attract it or an alternate manifestation of it.

For example many people who live in large cities fear getting robbed. They purchase the most expensive locks, and alarm systems, but they seem to attract those that would take from them in one form or another. At the very least, they have robbed themselves of freedom by locking their lives up so tightly. In either case, they have attracted what they fear.

Every day I go to the gym, and every day I put my pack with my keys, and other items in a locker without locking it. One day I was questioned by another member how I can do that. I simply told him that I believe in a positive human nature. I refuse to go through life fearing that someone is going to take my stuff. I have been going to the gym for four straight years and have never had anyone take anything. So many people fear the loss of things by others taking them. They don't realize that they are actually attracting that situation to themselves by their fears and attachment to material items.

Likewise if you love something and happily welcome it into your life, not from need but through shear passion and joy in how it will make all life better, you will open doors to these passions and attract them to you. You need not be attached to the manifestation of it, but see the feeling of joy that it may bring you and others around you.

The word passion has roots in many languages, here however, I am using it to mean "strong emotion, desire." Take a moment to think about anything in your life that you truly adore, whether it is a job, a house, or a person. You did not bring that into your life by a desperate need for it but more of a passionate desire or love for its presence or something similar to it. That is the law of attraction without attachment to the outcome. That is an example of using the concept of seeing through spirit.

The most important decision that we ever make is whether
we live in a friendly universe or a hostile universe
Albert Einstein

If we choose a hostile universe, which of course is ego-based, filled with competition, anger, emotional pain, hatred, and war, then we can only attract more of these things.

I think that if I were going to define, hell that would be a pretty reasonable definition.

The mirror image or compliment of this would be to choose a universe that is friendly. One that sees us all connected, and understands that the greatest way to live life is in service to the rest of this friendly universe. A world where the most powerful act we can perform is to raise others up.

If you want peace, then choose to think about peace. This is a universe whose foundation is love and spirituality. This obvious spirit-based life seems as a good start to define Heaven.

Fear is powerful, but love is more powerful, so it is just a matter of loving what you want more than fearing what you don't. By illumination, we embrace our fearful ego and it is healed.

> *Love is our highest word and a synonym for God*
> *Ralph Waldo Emerson*

I would expect to be in the presence of God if I find myself in Heaven...wouldn't you? Further, doesn't that mean that the more we love, the more Heaven-like we become?

It is important to realize that the manner in which we live is always a choice. The way that you respond to the gifts that come into your life is always your choice because you have free will. And the way that you respond to these gifts is determined by how you express your life.

Many people feel as though they will be happy if they can just get that job they have always wanted, or the spouse they have always had in their mind, or purchase the house of their dreams. They don't realize that joy and happiness is who you are. In joy, you attract joyful manifestations.

Are you grateful no matter what comes into your life? Can you see that even events in your life that may seem so terrible at the time, came to you as a response to your thoughts and passions, and are here to help you learn lessons and grow? They are all gifts, if you can only see them that way.

> *Intention triggers the transformation of energy and*
> *information, and organizes its own fulfillment*
> Deepak Chopra

Years ago, while I was teaching in Colorado, the priest at the church I attended had a very interesting way of looking at the difficulties in our lives:

> *When you feel pain, that's just God clearing away*
> *the dead unnecessary branches of our lives*
> Fr. James Koenigsfeld

Whenever I think about the most painful times of my life, I realize that those were the times of my greatest spiritual, emotional and intellectual development and am very grateful for those times. How you look at things is ALWAYS your choice.

Many of my years growing up were in a parochial school, and I distinctly remember a priest making a statement about free will:

> *No one can make you do ANYTHING...not even God*

That statement has stayed with me for many years. It has acted as a reminder that I decide what to accept into my life. I have always felt that everything in life happens for a reason. The key-determining factor of what we develop into is how we respond to the gifts of this life, and the continued gratitude and joy-expression of the celebration of life.

The ramifications of this thought process are staggering if you really think about it. How many people feel as though they are forced to do things in their lives?

Every day you choose to live an existence that is ego-based, or to live a life that is spirit-based, right here on earth. How can you do this? Do you focus on your physical existence, always comparing yourself to others on a superficial level? Do you focus on the spirit within, which sees that we are all one body of love? Therein lies the answer.

We have all known people that seem to be walking around with a storm cloud following them. They complain and never feel like they are getting any breaks. Every time something goes right, three things go wrong.

Then there are those that good things always seem to fall into their laps. They never seem concerned and are joyful to be around. Some say that it is easy to be happy when everything is going your way, when the truth is that things are attracted your way, when you bring out the joy and happiness of this existence.

It is your joy to look inside and answer the question. It's a tremendous journey. The truly amazing part of all of this is that no matter which thought process you choose, you must inevitably attract more of that, so you actually affect the world around you by the way that you think and feel.

Think long and hard before you choose, what it is that you wish to attract to your life. Do you attract loving spirit or fearful ego?

Some Of The Science Involved

Energy and information exist everywhere in
nature; at the level of pure consciousness, there is
nothing other than energy and information
Deepak Chopra
The Seven Spiritual Laws of Success

BEING A SCIENTIST, IT is not enough for me to accept things at face value, and while spirituality and its effects on the universe are fascinating ideas, I still need to see the possible mechanism for this process.

After studying the ideas of quantum physics for many years, tying that into what I already know about chemistry, and drawing the line between these concepts I have arrived at the belief that you can in fact cite scientific evidence that supports the idea that we, as spiritual beings are actually a part of a larger, and far greater source. This source is a "quantum neighborhood" from which we all originate, and whose power is at a level that is difficult if not impossible for our "human" minds to wrap around. While much of the evidence is circumstantial, and requires a degree of correlating, I feel as though this evidence helps us to understand some of the cosmic laws, such as the Law of Attraction, the Law of Pure Potentiality, the Law of Giving and Receiving, and many others.

All of these spiritual laws depend on similar resonating energies. From Chemistry and Quantum physics standpoint, this is where I tie the science into it.

The current science understanding of resonance frequency is as follows.

Unless any matter is at absolute zero, all molecules
and energy vibrate at a particular rate that
is specific to their particular makeup.

For so-called matter, such as molecules, the specific composition, and behavior has to do with the manner of electron configuration, the actual atoms and their masses, as well as the type of bond and the polarity.

Based on our model of atoms and molecules, when individual atoms come together to bond covalently, they often form a hybridized orbital that changes the configuration of the atoms based on electron repulsion. Additionally it changes the electron geometry, which has an effect on the electrostatic forces of the molecule as it interacts with the other molecules and the rest of the world. Both the molecular geometry and the electron geometry are based on a fundamental system of model building called the valence shell electron pair repulsion model (Called VSEPR).

These particular forces cause the molecules
to vibrate at a very specific frequency.

As I explain later in this chapter, energy waves also vibrate at a particular frequency. The frequency of waves is used as a means of identifying them on the electromagnetic spectrum. Each wave frequency is measurable and specific for each type of energy that science has identified. The known electromagnetic spectrum is illustrated later in this section.

This absolute zero is also called zero Kelvin, named after William Thomson Kelvin, a British mathematician and physicist who proposed in 1848 that all molecular motion, including vibrational motion ceases or nearly ceases at this temperature.

This temperature is calculated to be 273.15 degrees below zero centigrade, which is 460 degrees below, zero Fahrenheit.

*This means that even what we see as solid objects, like
this book, actually, are moving all of the time.*

Can you feel this? Is this vibration real? It is accepted to be scientifically sound based on its ability to be measured. It can be measured with the correct instruments, but, to the best of my knowledge, no humans have the physical sensitivity to detect it. Is it only real if we can feel it?

The generally accepted spectrum of <u>electromagnetic energy waves</u> is as follows from lowest energy and frequency to highest energy and frequency:

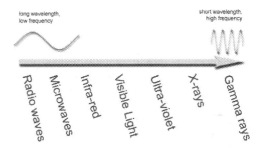

A miniature wave lesson is in order here: with regards to wave frequency, the higher the frequency, then the shorter the wavelength, which is the distance from crest to crest of one wave to another. Alternatively, the lower frequency wave is produced by a longer wavelength of that particular electromagnetic energy.

*As a rule of thumb the higher frequencies
carry with them a higher energy level and the
lower frequencies carry a lower energy.*

This is why we do not generally become concerned when being constantly bombarded with radio waves, on a daily basis, but over exposure to X-ray or gamma waves can be very disconcerting; not to mention, ionizing.

Tying wave frequency in with resonance frequency of a molecule, if the frequency of molecular vibrations is slower than the frequency of the energy oscillations, then the energy passes through the molecule sometimes by damaging the molecule, and sometimes not. However if the molecule is vibrating at a frequency faster than the energy striking it, the energy is absorbed or reflected by the molecule, in the same way that greenhouse gases allow UV light to pass through from the sun but absorb the infrared energy as it tries to escape the planet. Sometimes the passing through can do great damage as in the case of gamma radiation penetrating human flesh.

Sound wave energy is known to test at a slower frequency than those in the electromagnetic spectrum, which is why you see a batter hit a ball from a distance before you can hear the crack of the bat making contact with the ball.

Quantum physics has taken this concept quite a bit further. There appear to be energies that are slower then the ones mentioned in the electromagnetic spectrum above and sound. These are matter energies.

The concept is that matter is just energy slowed down enough so that our senses perceive them to be solid, liquid, or gas, through a combination of appropriate repulsion and attraction forces.

Our body's energy frequency matches that of other "matter" and they collide. The interaction of attractive and repulsive forces then gives us the perception of the matter being solid, liquid or gas, etc. Can it be taken farther?

*The body is NOT solid matter, which was evidenced by
the resurrection of Jesus' body. His ability to command
the cosmic energy of atoms not only allowed his own
resurrection but that of his friend Lazarus.*
Michel Bernard Beckwith
Spiritual Liberation

This may seem far-fetched but theoretical quantum physics has support for this very reality.

Brian Greene is a Physicist with Columbia University and has perpetuated the idea of energy being the makeup of all matter. This energy vibrates in the form of string bands. These bands of energy string are smaller than subatomic particles called protons, neutrons and electrons. They are smaller still than particles that make up subatomic particles, called quarks. This has lead to the quantum theory of strings. He explains this concept in great detail in The Elegant Universe.

*The bottom line is that, according to this theory, which is
supported mathematically, all matter is actually energy.*

Many would say that this is not science because it cannot be observed and is not testable. By the definition of scientific hypothesis this is true, but it does open the door of possibilities.

Remember that if one energy is vibrating slower than another, then it will not pass through, giving the feeling of their being matter.

The Minds Vibrational Effect

There is growing anecdotal evidence that Yogi masters have tapped into the ability to control these vibrations through meditation and have actually walked through walls or levitated. Again, we may scoff at the ideas because we have not witnessed it or experienced it. Does that make it unreal?

> *On the subatomic level, there is no causal mechanism*
> *in the universe... So-called random binary processes*
> *could be predicted, even influenced...* <u>*What appeared*</u>
> <u>*to put a halt to randomness was a living observer*</u>
> *Lynn McTaggart*
> *The Field*

Did you catch that? It was the observer's presence and interaction of actually observing that may have caused a random process to occur one way versus another.

The Heisenberg uncertainty principle states that it is impossible to know both the position and momentum of an electron simultaneously.

> *That is to say that all matter is simply waves of*
> *possibilities until it is measured through observation.*

We don't need a ruler to measure. We measure by simply looking or listening. When we do so, we give it physical reality, and so a wave of possibility takes on a position of reality.

Quantum physics seems to be coming up with more and more evidence that matter is not solid at all, but in fact, is energy with constant flux of energy flows (waves) interacting with each other. It is US, the observers that make matter "real."

Lynne McTaggart's book, <u>The Field: The quest for the Secret Force of the Universe</u> discusses the idea of absolute zero but goes much deeper into the ideas that are shaping quantum physics today with regards to this temperature at which all molecular motion ceases. While I cannot do her book justice, I found it fascinating that McTaggart re-proposes such concepts as zero-point energy. This is an unlimited source of instantaneous energy found at absolute zero. At our current state of science, this is simply theoretical since we cannot achieve absolute zero, however the possibilities are extraordinary. Is it possible that this limitless and instantaneous source of energy could exist if we can't detect it with our current technology? Remember that John Dalton's proposal of the existence of small balls of matter in his atomic model was just a theory based on circumstantial evidence until the technology came along and found a way to measure it.

It is widely accepted by all camps of physics and chemistry that 99.9 percent of an atom is empty space, and yet we feel the effect of atom constantly. Think about that for a moment...

> *99.9 percent of atoms, which means molecules, which means tissue, organs, cells, bodies, tables, chairs, cars, everything that we call "real" is actually mostly empty space.*

For the moment we will stay with more traditional Newtonian, and Einsteinian based physics, although the field of Quantum physics is also very widely accepted.

The understood interaction of matter (anything which has mass and takes up space) with energy is that increased waves exposed to matter can affect it. An example of this is how sunlight or ultraviolet energy excites the molecules in ice to turn it to liquid which we call melting or directly from ice to water vapor which we call sublimation. These are interactions that we have evidence of with energies that we have familiarity with. What about energies that we don't, yet have the ability to detect or measure yet?

There appear to be energies that move much faster than those mentioned in the previous electromagnetic spectrum.

Physics has utilized numerous calculations to develop the concept that thoughts and, indeed feelings have their own energy, which moves so quickly that current instruments cannot measure them, but the human consciousness can.

Further, it is determined that negative thoughts and feelings have a lower and slower energy than those of positive, spiritual thoughts and feelings. In other words that there are levels of different energy patters within each grouping.

This is actually supported by David Hawkins Book: <u>Power Versus Force.</u> Hawkins demonstrates, using scientific method and thousands of test cases that negative thoughts and feelings make us weaker than positive thoughts and feelings, by using a technique called applied kinesiology.

What is fascinating and correlates with known energies is that these energies attract similar resonating energies to each other. So high energies with positive feelings attract more positive feelings, and slower energies of negative feelings attract more of the same. Does this sound like the law of attraction?

Let's not forget that the atom was once thought to be the smallest particle that could exist until protons, neutrons, and electrons were thought to be the absolute smallest particle possible. With the advent of super- colliders we now have evidence that smaller particles exist which are called quarks. As stated above string theory is a branch of quantum physics that postulates that even smaller packages exist but that they are energy not matter. Nothing is real until it is.

Does this sound incongruent with the "real" world? How can energy exist if we cannot measure it? Take, as an example, the reality that the human consciousness is measuring light energy at every turn. When the human eye perceives colors, they are not colors per se, but the energy waves at a particular frequency, which your mind interprets as a particular color. Yet you trust that when you see red, that it IS red, or blue, and so on. Additionally, due to the fact that the back of the eye is concave, the images that are projected to the light sensing cones and rods are actually upside down. It is our mind that flips them back upside right. All in the "blink of an eye." Actually it occurs faster than that.

If you use your eyes to measure these energies, then it is not really a stretch of human imagination to think that you may perceive other levels of energy, which may be at a more subconscious level, and with instruments (senses) that we are not aware of.

This is confirmed in Wayne Dyers, <u>The Power of Intention</u>. Dyer goes on to report about five levels of energy. They are as follows:

1. Matter-energy whose frequency is so slow that is blocks or absorbs other energies which come in contact with it. This is probably due to electron repulsion.
2. Sound- These waves of energy are faster, compression waves and can be felt by the appropriate sensors (such as ear drums).
3. Light-These energy waves are represented and expanded in the electro magnetic spectrum in the previous chart.
4. Thought- These energy waves can be tested and calibrated very easily through muscle testing. Dr. David Hawkins book, *Power vs Force*, goes into great detail on this topic as well as the next one.
5. Spirit-This is the fastest of all energies and moves instantaneously across the universe.

Consider that energy is around you at all times. These are energies that scientists have tested and generated for decades. All of the waves in the electromagnetic spectrum have been quantified and utilized in every way imaginable by the human mind. Yet the only frequency that we perceive with our eyes is the visible light spectrum of energy, which is the smallest of energy spectrums among the electromagnetic energies. Are the others not real because you cannot see them?

For us to believe that we have already reached the pinnacle of scientific understanding of energy is the very definition of scientific arrogance.

Read each word below separately and notice
how each one makes you feel.
Love
Kindness
Pride
Patriotism
Anger
Terror
Excitement

As you read this list of words, were you not affected differently by each word instantaneously? Isn't that what energy does? Isn't that real?

These can be calculated and predicted. Ask yourself if you have ever walked into a room and immediately perceived the emotions of the room, be they jovial or tense. Is it not possible that this is a part of our connection to the divine and interconnectedness?

The more pertinent question is, do you accept your ability to perceive these through some unknown spiritual meter or do you simply ignore it and eventually mask your ability to do so?

Based on the understandings of chemistry and theoretical
quantum physics, we are really just a complex and
organized, yet chaotic orchestra of energy.

That may be an over simplification, but it is truth at the rudimentary level. This leads us back into areas of zero-point energy. Evidence of this energy can be found in the fact that electrons remain constant over time. If you understand that atoms have charges, and we understand that matter eventually loses charges over time, then why doesn't electron charge dissipate? Based on the same concepts in magnetism as they lose their electrostatic force over time, electrons should lose theirs as well. McTaggart believes that this is because they are moving across a barrier found at absolute zero, and each time they do, they are recharged by zero-point energy.

Why is it that electrons and atoms seem to pop in and out of existence? This can be measured. Where do they go? Where do they get their energy? There is a far greater discussion here that I am only skimming over but the point is, that science and the scientific approach must apply to all things or it is not valid.

So if science applies to some energy, then it must apply to other forms as well, and while we do not have a direct means of measuring all of this at this moment, the model fits! It is therefore, NOT out of the realm of possibility that all matter, including us, is energy and therefore may be affected by the interaction of various forms of energy.

Evidence for this existence

... Your cosmic identity is made in the image and likeness of love, intelligence, compassion, joy, creativity and beauty itself
Michael Bernard Beckwith

Intuition:

HAVE YOU EVER BEEN faced with a very important decision and either of two different directions seemed viable? There are people that will tell you to write down the pros and cons of each and decide that way. Now that is some real ego world thinking.

I have found that when faced with these decisions, the answer lies deep down inside. It seems that the best path is being directed toward you if you only listen to the inner voice called your intuition. It is there if you are quiet enough to hear, feel it and not too busy writing down pros and cons. Further, it is there as a result of your source energy directing you. Invariably, if you follow that path, things will unfold in a blessed and often miraculous manner.

How do you make spontaneous right choices? By paying attention to the sensations of comfort or discomfort in your body... For some people the message of comfort or discomfort is in the area of the solar plexus, but for most it's in the area of the heart... You will know the answer is right because it will feel right, without any lingering doubts
Deepak Chopra
The Seven Spiritual Laws of Success

The statement by Deepak Chopra is one that I have felt for as long as I have been making choices and as long as I have been advising my students on right choices.

To understand this statement by Deepak it is necessary to gain some basic understanding about Chakras. Chakra is an ancient Sanskrit word. There are seven Chakras in the body and are the centers of our spiritual power and a means to connect to our true self as well as source.

I find it interesting that the area of the solar plexus is the location of the third Chakra. This is the area of the body responsible for picking up vibrations form people, places and things. In other words, this area helps us sense appropriate and inappropriate frequencies of resonance. This is also the area involved with personal power, self-control and the related emotions of self-acceptance. Can you see how this ties into intuition? If your third Chakra were receiving vibrations from others and combining this with your own personal power, you would be receiving information about senders of high or low frequency energy and matching it to your own inner source power.

The second area and the area that Chopra feels is the most common area for intuitive choices is the heart area. This is the area of the body where the forth Chakra is located. It is also the Chakra responsible for the connection between our physical, ego and spiritual body. The spiritual body is our connection to the universe. What better way is there to know if a choice is an appropriate one for the entire universe than through this area of the body? It is truly your source connection.

Attracting high or low energy to our lives
*You can be afraid of the future or know in
your heart, that the best is yet to come
Cannon Robertson*

As a high school teacher, I see students who reflect both of these ideas. There is a difference between spiritually living for the present and egoically living with the expectation of impending doom. Fear is always ego-based, because spirit is connected to source. How can we be afraid of source?

Those that live for the moment are filled with and attract joy. They bring that same joy to everyone around them. They savor what they are experiencing in the moment, and everyone around them can feel it.

Those that see only the doom in life exude and attract negative, slow moving energy, and can quickly bring others into this thought and feeling pattern. It is not always visible to the naked eye, but just spending a few moments in their presence makes this abundantly clear. Not only do they speak only negatives about their lives, they actually broadcast this slow-moving energy to all around.

As Cannon Robertson's quote implies, there are people that fear the future, in fact there are those that feel that there is no future. They, often have given up on a future in this world, and have begun to shut down into depression, anxiety, and eventually they attract their own death by attracting fatal disease or accidental death. Much of the depression of this world comes from this perspective and that triggers the requisite chemical imbalances that we respond to by taking a myriad of pills to counteract. None of these ever address the problem only help to temporarily hold back the symptoms.

We all know people who move about this world seemingly with a storm cloud over their head. Their life is gloom and doom. They have an uncanny ability to see the negative in every situation, and never realize that all things happen as a means of growth and development. Their cloud can be so dark and heavy that they can affect others around them in the same way, simply by being in their presence.

If you know people like this, try not to judge them. They are working on their own lessons. Simply bless them with love, whenever you are around them, and pray for their enlightenment. You cannot become enlightened for them. They must seek out answers to their own questions when the time is right, and they must forgive themselves. You can be available to them when they see this time in their life, but you cannot live it for them. Additionally, you need to be careful about being in that low energy with them for extended periods. This can have an adverse effect on you as well, and you may find yourself edging toward more fearful egoism in an effort to empathize with them. Don't get caught up in that.

On the other side of this future coin, there are those that not only savor the present, but also relish the idea of a future of interaction and love with all of creation. These people seem to have an innate ability to attract good fortune and happiness into their lives. These are people that make others feel better simply by their presence. These are people that know that by giving of themselves, they are actually blessed. They roll with changes, in fact they welcome the adventure associated with change in their lives, and see all change as good.

The person who sees the present as a blessing and always views life's circumstances as something that they attracted to themselves as a means to grow, learn and develop into a more enlightened, God-like, loving spiritual energy are a welcome energy to be around. It is a joy to meet people who literally savor every moment in life. It is said that God is love. I could not agree more. Therefore to love more is to be more God-like. Remember that you and everyone else were created in Gods image.

You are a piece of God
Wayne Dyer
Power of Intention

53

When you think and feel this way about yourself and everyone else around you, it certainly enhances the way that you see the world. Remember that EVERYONE is created this way. It is only the choices that each person makes in the way they view their "real" world that dictate whether they see themselves as God-like, and treat the world in a spiritual way or an ego-based victim-like manner.

Dr. Dyer goes farther with this idea and viewing the world with special lenses, which filter out the structure and material world that holds all of our ego-centered adornments. These lenses look only at the spiritual energy of creation.

> *What you notice is pure love vibrating before*
> *your eyes. You see enormous strands of peaceful*
> *glimmering energy connecting each of us*
> *Wayne Dyer*
> *Being in Balance*

What amazing insight and what a glorious way to look at life. How can we hate or compete with or be at war with those that are connected to us? How could we possibly harm those that we see the light of God in? It seems obvious when you look at life this way that we all belong and that we are all part of an intricate dance of celebration and life. We only need to see through the proper lenses.

Finding Peace Through Meditation and Yoga:

> *I mean the whole thing about meditation and yoga is*
> *about connecting to the higher part of yourself, and then*
> *seeing that every living thing is connected in some way*
> *Gillian Anderson*
> *Actress, Philanthropist, Buddhist*

Meditation and yoga may be the best avenues for us to look in and be present to the true self. For most, the average day consists of waking up early, perhaps drinking some coffee, eating some form of breakfast, and shuffling off to work. While at our "job" we are busily handling all of the day-to-day duties until it is time to go home. A great many Americans, then go about watching television mindlessly to all hours of the night, and then going off to bed to repeat this cycle.

This cycle is one that ultimately will lead to high levels of stress and spiritual bankruptcy. While it may bring some pleasures into your life, such as boats and motorcycles, or fancy clothing, these will NEVER fill the gaping hole where the true self is missing. The natural state of the true self is joyful and happy, but you must look inside to find it.

> *Pleasure is temporary, fleeting, whereas happiness is a constant*
> *Michael Bernard Beckwith*
> *The Answer is You*

There is no room in this cycle for the process of introspection. There is little, if any time to listen to the silence and find our source. Meditation is a process that, when inserted into our lives, can help us all ground to what is truly "real."

There are a great many forms of meditation, and I am no master, but I have been meditating since I was thirteen. In that time, I have tried many levels of meditation. I have always had trouble balancing the need for it with the time that it takes and finding a good time of day to be successful with it.

It has taken time, and reading a great many masters of this process, but I feel that I have pieced together a method of meditation which is both spiritually and temporally effective. I cannot say that it will work for you but it is a process that I have met with success in my life.... when I take the time to exercise it.

This is a combination of techniques from some of the greatest masters of meditation. If you only perform and focus on one of these steps for twenty minutes, you will find great benefit. It is important to find a way to be present to yourself and quiet your mind on a daily basis.

Here are the steps that I use:

1. Sit in an upright comfortable position, in an area free of sensory distraction.

2. Close your eyes, and focus only on the process of your breath moving in and out of your body. Think only of the steady constant flow of air molecules moving in and out.

3. As you breath, visualize yourself as simply becoming a part of the whole universe. See your body simply disappearing and the spiritual energy of love being all that exists, and you, a part of that loving universe.

4. After 5 minutes or however long it takes to quiet the mind, bring a spirit thought of love, beauty, joy, etc to your mind.

5. As you sit beside this word, notice, other thoughts that come to your mind, and watch them in your minds eye as they pass by. If you get stuck on a thought, simply refocus on your spirit word and let it float down beside you again.

6. As the thoughts related to your spirit word begin to dissipate, begin to see through your third eye Chakra. This is physically located between your eyes and slightly elevated from there.

7. As you peer through this Chakra, send out your feeling of love and joy to the universe for a few minutes

8. Finally, re-center by focusing on your breath again for a minute or two as you begin to move around and gently open your eyes.

As a follow up to the procedure above, it should be noted that you may simply choose any one step above and repeat it for the twenty minute period of time, and still reap great benefits from this. In other words, any one of the above steps is its own, stand-alone meditation.

Admittedly, I do not always make the time to do this, and I can notice the difference when I don't. I am less patient with my students, more irritable, more tired, and I can even feel more persecuted. When I do attend to my meditative practice, I clearly sense the true self, the spiritual connection to source that we are all a part of. Some call this the ghost in the machine. The more that you illuminate this true self through your own awareness, the more that you emanate this to those around you and the more that you attract others that do the same.

In my opinion, there is very little, in life that is not evolved in a more spiritual manner than by the process of meditation. It is not a chore. Think of it as visiting your neighbor, who just happens to be the "real" you.

The evidence for existence that I have discussed in this section is subtle and that is the way that it should be. While science may be able to provide circumstantial evidence for the presence of the true self, and a means of supporting the ideas of spirituality, there is nothing that hands this to you on a silver platter. There is no irrefutable, rock solid evidence.

That being said, we always have a choice in the way that we view our lives and those around us. Deep inside me, I KNOW the truth: That we all connected, that we are all here to serve each other in the most powerful energy in the universe… Love

Section 3:
Application

The following chapters apply the Ego "real" World and Spirit "real" World concepts to several topics and view. A great many quotes are utilized to illustrate that the thought process is universal among some of the greatest spiritual thinkers in the world. Further, there are suggestions as to one or two methods that may help us all to arrive at turning points between the two perspectives for those that are interested.

Environment/Ecology

Let us a little permit Nature to take her own way;
she better understands her own affairs than we
Michel de Montaigne
French Writer 1533-1592

TRUE SPIRITUAL EVOLUTION ALWAYS enhances its surroundings. As a species of organism on this planet, we are destroying resources and other species at a far faster rate than can be replenished.

Between 20000-27000 species of organisms are lost every year according to estimates by many experts in the field. Some experts predict the loss of over 20% of the species of our planet by 2022, due to habitat loss, climate change, competition for food and water. Does this sound like spiritual evolution?

The United States leads the world in consumption of oil, electricity, natural gas, and corn just to name a few (mintlife.com 2009), yet we have only 4.5 percent of the world population. Most Americans are not aware of the amount of deprivation across the globe because they are kept from its view.

It does not take a genius to calculate out the long-term effects of this life style. There are those people that take the perspective that we can use up the resources without replenishing them and without being good stewards of the large rock we call earth. This perspective has obvious implications for the future of our planet and the generations that follow. It appears, however, that shortsightedness and pursuit of material wealth seem to determine what level of responsibility that people in decision-making roles will take.

It may be the developer that strips the land, the oil company executive that drains the oil from pristine lands and then refines that oil to increase the amount of pollutant in the atmosphere. It may be the logging company clear cutting a forest with out replenishing the trees. The cause is so often centered on financial gain over responsibility.

> *All things share the same breath - the beast, the tree, the*
> *man... the air shares its spirit with all the life it supports.*
> *Humankind has not woven the web of life. We are but*
> *one thread within it. Whatever we do to the web, we do to*
> *ourselves. All things are bound together. All things connect*
> *Chief Seattle Duwamish tribe*

What I find so amazing about Chief Seattle's insights are found in this statement:

> *Whatever we do to the web, we do to ourselves. All*
> *things are bound together. All things connect*

Species disappear on a daily basis, not only due to deforestation but ALL habitat destruction, be it land, sea, or air. It is important to remember that not only what is good for you is good for me, but also what is good for ALL life is good for us.

The pendulum of consumerism to conservationism tends to swing wide. In the seventies and eighties, issues like the greenhouse effect, the hole in the ozone, deforestation, overpopulation, over-using resources, de-speciation, etc appeared to be at the forefront of our society. With the exception of the ozone hole, these have recently taken an alarming turn. This has illustrated, clearly, that lack of responsible care for these issues will ultimately lead to devastating consequences for all life.

Let's focus on the global warming issue. I realize that this has emerged as a polarizing political issue, but I will do my level best to take the politics out of the issue.

Concerned activists such as Al Gore in the producing of <u>An Inconvenient Truth</u> have brought this issue back into the picture. The ever-growing haze that can be seen over cities is a daily reminder that this issue is in our world and must be addressed. Nation-wide heat waves, intensified, and increased frequency of hurricanes and tornadoes, increased disease, melting polar ice caps, are a few of the effects of turning a blind eye to this issue. These are not the ravings of environmental extremists. Scientists all over the planet concur on this topic.

The National Oceanic and Atmospheric Administration (NOAA. Gov) has stated that this past year (2011) has been the most extreme year for weather anomalies, such as tidal waves, hurricanes, and tornadoes. All of these have increased in both frequency and intensity according to NOAA. Climate-change models predicted all of these, decades ago. I am a science teacher and look for evidence that I can observe. It's all there. All you have to do is look. I encourage all people to look deeply on this issue, and not just listen to political figureheads.

> *A large body of evidence supports the conclusion*
> *that human activity is the primary driver of recent*
> *warming. This evidence has accumulated over*
> *several decades, and from hundreds of studies*
> *National Oceanic and Atmospheric Administration*

It is "real" science. Since the average amount of CO_2 (the major greenhouse gas) emitted per gallon of gas is approximately twenty pounds, it just makes sense to use our technology to increase gas mileage and produce vehicles that produce little to zero greenhouse gasses (and get better gas mileage which saves money). We can no longer simply assume that these gases will simply be diluted adequately into the atmosphere.

For those that feel that this is a normal earth cycle that is unaffected by mans activities, it is true that the earth has gone through cycles of heating and cooling in its geologic history, however geologic records indicate that these cyclical patterns have occurred over thousands of years and can be explained by levels of plant vegetation, and other factors such as massive volcanic eruptions. The recent increase in temperature, which is not in dispute by any reputable scientists, has occurred in a matter of a few decades and is directly correlated with the increase of green house gasses, primarily carbon dioxide, which is also not in dispute by any reputable scientists.

These numbers really help to put the effects in to perspective. According to the United States department of Energy, it takes approximately 1.5 gallons of crude oil to make a gallon of gasoline.

In a May 3, 2004 article in the Seattle Times, Americans used almost 9 million barrels (42 gallons in a barrel) of crude oil in 2003...DAILY!! This number had reflected an increase in use of 1.6% annually over the previous five years, right about the time that the large SUVs started to become so popular in the United States.

Some quick math indicates that 378 million gallons of oil used daily, and 283.5 million gallons of gasoline used which resulted in 5.678 billion pounds of carbon dioxide released by American cars in one DAY! I don't bring these numbers to light for any reason other than the reason of bringing a genuine realization of this issue. The math does not lie.

There are, of course, other reasons to stop or decrease drilling for oil. The Exxon Valdez spill in 1989 was devastating to wildlife in Prince William Sound and is still being cleaned up to this day.

At this point we still do not know the total impact of the BP oil spill in 2010. Approximately five million barrels of crude oil spilled into the ocean and will have devastating impacts on wildlife, tourism and American jobs for decades. This occurred because of the prioritization for material possession over the necessity to be a good steward of our planet.

We have the technology to develop alternative sources of energy, which are clean, safe and VERY effective. Why have we not done that? Who benefits from us remaining under the umbrella of oil as our primary source of energy? Why would anyone in their right mind not want to improve their lives while improving the planet at the same time? Oil dependency is only one area that grossly impacts our environment.

Between the use of resources and destruction of habitat, this planet cannot mathematically be sustained. The world population is estimated to be nine billion by 2050. What choices will we all make to change this unsustainable lifestyle?

Ego "real" World

Most ego-based lives do not understand the value of recycling or reusing resources. They are incapable of seeing the value of preserving a species of frog in the Amazon rainforest, or flower in the Pacific Northwest, or a wolf in Sonoran Desert. The person that sees himself as a separate entity and is identified by what they own, does not see the relevance between themselves and these "outside" entities.

Many people in this category may feel that this is not an issue for them, since this may not become critical for several years. They simply don't see how the loss of a species of organism or a few more pounds of CO_2 can have any impact on them. They see the destruction of an Alaskan forest as being fine as long as it keeps the gas prices down.

Over the last several years, exceptionally large vehicles have become a sign of status for the ego world. These of course use even more oil and compound problems. Sadly, these people define themselves by what they have or how much power they wield in the ego world. They, unfortunately, see the physical world around them as having been put there to serve their desires. If this means the loss of habitats that lead to extinctions of living creatures, then this seems acceptable. It is all about survival of the fittest.

There is an inability to draw the connection between preservation of species and sustainable use of resources and themselves. They seem to see the use and disposal of resources and other living organisms as what they are entitled to. At the very least, they may have turned a blind eye to these situations, and certainly do not see it as their responsibility. They would like to make a difference but it seems to be just too much effort.

Spirit "real" World

People, who live the spirit-life, understand what the enlightened Chief Seattle meant by his insightful statement:

> *Whatever we do to the web, we do to ourselves. All things are bound together. All things connect*

In this realm, they see that by not only preserving but also enhancing other living organisms lives, including other humans, they are, themselves, enhanced.

They understand that dealing with global climate change is important, not only for our existence, but because it is the ethical thing to do. That in protecting our environment, we protect other living organisms, <u>and all life is enhanced!</u>

They "get" that a sustainable planet is one that is not stressed by overuse of resources and over-polluted by our waste simply to increase their social status, but is one that we live in harmony with the entire planet itself as one. In this same way, spiritually led people see that we are all one with it and each other.

They feel better simply by picking up a piece of trash or reusing a plastic bag, or recycling paper, or giving to environmental/ecological causes. Their lives are enhanced by these simple acts, and can actually perceive the damage to the connection when they are not able to do so.

This goes beyond simple common sense of foretelling that if we use up all our resources that there will be nothing left to use.

This speaks to a "knowing" that by caring for our environment, protecting other species and their habitats, conserving our resources, that we are showing respect and love for life. There is no life that is more significant than another. It is all sacred. Caring for our environment and the life contained in it brings us closer to source.

In other words we are being more God-like.

<u>Turning Point</u>

Try to pick up a piece of trash and throw it away or recycle a can and NOT feel better. It can't be done. If you look deep inside, you will feel how good these simple acts are because you know that it brings all of humanity closer to a more evolved state.

Today, in some way, help preserve a life that you have no apparent relationship to. You can do this by giving to worthy causes, working at the humane society, or through several charities designed at protection and development of life.

When you preserve life, when you clean up the environment
and protect those that need help, you are recognizing the
spirit inside you and the connection that we all have.

You may allow pride to enter in and become annoyed that you are picking up after other people, or that you are giving to people that should be able to do things for themselves, but if you look deep into the spirit, you will know that you have enhanced this life. Remember that pride is an ego state.

This is more than simply doing the "right" thing. Right and wrong are judgments...it goes back to the enhancement and evolution of the spirit which feeds the connection to all of life. Material status just for the sake of status moves us away from spirit and creates more separation from others. When material status is brought about by the parasitism of the world around us, we lose more. We sacrifice our soul connection.

> *The point of life is the fabrication of the soul*
> *Thomas Moore*
> *Care of the Soul*

When we endeavor to sustain, and enhance this world, we gain a wealth far greater than any material resource. Caring for the living organisms as well as the environment they thrive in is one of the best ways to do so. Some times, even science fiction movies have it right.

> *Spock (regarding the impending extinction of humpback*
> *whales): To hunt a species to extinction is not logical*
> *Gillian (Whale Caretaker): Whoever*
> *said the human race was logical?*
> *Star-trek IV: The Voyage Home*

I challenge you to act logically and spiritually intelligent with regard to our environment and the life it contains.

What are some specific things that you can do? Give to needy environmental causes or conservation organizations. There are many to choose from. For every simple act in this direction you will feel better in your true self. After time, you will want to do more and more. Knowing that what you are doing is helping so many lives, is a great feeling.

You can do simple things like turning off lights when not in use, picking up trash, separating recycling, composting. You can do very elaborate things as well, like donating time, money, and effort.

There are a number of places that you can go to for information on this. Instead of watching the news and all that is wrong, get involved in helping the world evolve. There is a lot to feel good about out there. You just need to point yourself in the right direction.

> *This is a beautiful planet with beautiful*
> *loving and caring people*
> *Proclaim this truth every day*
> *Lonnie C. Edwards MD*
> *Spiritual Laws That Govern Humanity and the Universe*

If everyone woke up and proclaimed this every day, how different would this planet look? How much better would our quality of life be globally?

Remember that this world is home for all life, and it is spiritually intelligent to care for it the best way that we can. If you follow your connection, you will see the happiness that is generated to you and the world around you, in service to all. Treat all life as sacred

Human Interaction

Why are you afraid? Because you believe that you are
neither loveable nor capable of loving another
… All negativity in your life will fall away as you
undo this simple erroneous belief about yourself
Paul Ferrini
Love Without Conditions

Seperation

WHEN YOU ARE WALKING down the street and you make eye contact with someone else, what do you do? Do you look away? Do you stare them down? Do you smile and warmly say hello? Each of those is a different approach to the same situation.

The way we interact with each other is significant in what it says about what is in our heart.

It seems to me that many people prefer to remain in their shells and not reach out to those around them. I believe that, to many, this is a "safe" way to live. But is it? Is it safer to perpetuate the idea that we are separate and that we are all competing for our piece of the pie, or are we better off viewing the universe as friendly and that we are all from the same place? Which perspective makes you feel better?

As a high school teacher, I have been especially aware of how people have retreated into their shells, because that may feel "safer" to them. Although this is not, in any way, limited to high schools, it is certainly concentrated there. These are young adults that are trying to learn their way and assert who they are.

In recent years with the advent of cell phones, and MP3 players, high school students in particular but a growing number of people in public have visible excuses not to interact with those around them. On any given high school campus there are hundreds or even thousands of young people within one foot of each other, most with their cell phones stuck on their ear or texting or ear buds from a game or ipod.

Regardless of the tool, there they stand within inches of human interaction, but are completely cutoff from what is occurring around them.

In addition to teenagers retreating at the schools, there are growing numbers of students that are home-schooled each year. According to the US Department of Education (source: IES, National Center for Educational Statistics), there were 1.5 Million students in the US, ages 5-17 years old, which were home schooled in 2007. This is truly regression into the shell of a protected environment.

On any given day, in a local coffee shop the vast majority of the people, often including myself, are busily working on laptops or playing on game devices, or text messaging someone. At the same time they ignore the people that are within their reach. This not an anomaly… this is the norm.

One day after working out in the gym, I walked into the sauna and there were four other people in there. Two men clearly knew each other but were not interacting; instead they were text messaging. Another woman was talking on her cell phone while she had her ipod ear buds in… Did I mention that this was in the sauna? The other woman in there was simply sitting quietly. As we made eye contact, I smiled and we began to interact by talking to each other…imagine that.

I walked away from this encounter amused, confused, dismayed, and exhilarated. I found it amusing that people would be so attached to electronic devices that they felt the need to bring them into the sauna with them. I was confused on how people who were clearly friends would spend so much time with the figurative wall of exclusion around themselves when they could have been interacting with each other. I must admit that I was dismayed that five people could be in such proximity and the majority of the people were afraid to interact with those around them.

I call this the elevator syndrome. If you have ever ridden an elevator with several other unacquainted people you understand this. A number of people all within a couple of feet and most of them are afraid to even make eye contact, let alone carry a conversation. I was exhilarated at the one other interaction that I did have in the sauna. We shared a moment of time together. No one can ever take that away.

I have always been fascinated by this phenomenon. How can we be so close to each other and not be a part of each other's lives? We come from the same source, yet we act as if we have nothing to share. I can honestly say, that whenever I have truly paid attention, everyone I have interacted with and been present to, has had an effect on my life. But we must be present to each other. We must see each other as all parts of the same spirit instead of separate egos.

How would a person be viewed if they went about on their daily interaction with everyone they came in contact and each encounter resulted in them smiling and saying:

"Hello, how are you? It is nice to see you."

Imagine the response to such a person as they warmly struck conversation with everyone around them. More often than not many people might look upon this person as strange or even dangerous. Parents might even shield their children from such a person in public. Many of us have become fearful and even angry with everyone else in society, because we look at each other as individuals, individuals that are in competition.

My piece of the pie

I will be referring to this again in other sections, but as a high school teacher, I have noticed an increased sense of entitlement among youth. I see it as a teacher but more so as a club sports coach. This is the "I deserve" mentality. This has become prevalent among the students I teach and players that I coach and becomes perpetuated as adults. There was a time, not that long ago, that a need to earn what you have through hard work and appropriate behavior was far more pervasive. This entitlement, in my opinion, has bled over into the way that we view the world, and is, of course, a manifestation of the ego.

> *Rule 2: The world won't care about your self-esteem. The world will expect you to accomplish something before you feel good about yourself*
> *Charles Sykes (educator)*
> *Eleven Things You'll Never Learn in School*
> *Dumbing Down our Kids*

As a result of our belief in separation and self-entitlement, there is constant competition on the road, in the grocery store lines, and at the ATM. Small areas such as elevators truly convey our discomfort with this. We all come from the same source and yet we cannot even acknowledge each other's existence. Most religions, somewhere in their scripture recognition, edify each other as brothers and sisters. Do we always treat each other this way?

How many people have died because of fear of others? Fear and anger have been driving forces in religious, social, and political deaths over many decades. Gang violence, hate crimes, assassinations of great and peaceful leaders like Mohandas Gandhi, Martin Luther King, mass genocide, world wars.

Unfortunately this list is endless. These are hardly the actions of a loving a spiritually based life. How much different would this list look if we all recognized that we have a common source?

Ego "real" World

In the Ego world, people are separate and in competition with each other for parking spaces, pole positions on the road, money, athletics, and territory. Those not wishing to compete seclude themselves as best they can by home schooling, and non-interaction. If you don't see this, look at what happens when people simply bump into each other, or find each other on the road competing for a streetlight.

It is our egos that keep us separate from each other; our egos keep us "protected." The ego world equates that in order to get ahead, someone else must fall behind us. Our personal space must not be invaded; our comfort zone must not be breeched. When these things happen, people will often do anything in order to put things back in "order." Often they will completely avoid eye contact, or do their best to avoid being around people. They may simply become completely engrossed in their electronics, or books just to stay in their bubble. The competitive lengths that people go to on a sports field can be very surprising. I have known coaches that will "bend" the rules or even put kids in harms way just to win a game. This approach is one of complete individualism.

Those driven by ego seem to believe that the only way that they can succeed is if someone else loses, because there is a finite amount of ego-based stuff, and they want "their fair share."

The following is a true story about a dorm-mate that I had in college. He was fresh out of the Marines and had a very powerful personality. He once told me that he goes into bars looking to get into fights. This was his advice:

> *"What you do, is catch some other guys eyes and*
> *stare him down. If he doesn't look away, you go*
> *over and ask him what his problem is."*

What was he competing for? This is the epitome of ego and pride at its pinnacle of existence. I only hope that he found more spirit in life. It saddens me to think how he lived his life back then. He is certainly not the only person that feels that fighting is somehow fulfilling. What he did not get back then is that this approach was simply a fear-tactic of the ego to keep him from looking inside at the authentic self.

When I look at the sports world and all of the different types of violence in sports, I am disheartened. While I still watch football, I am taken aback at the level of violence that even it has taken on. Instead of competing in the spirit of the games, players constantly partake in a series of one-up-manship on an individual basis. This leads to constant individual ego-centrism.

I try to never watch truly violent sports, but occasionally I will be at a sports bar and catch glimpses of "cage-fighting and Mixed Martial Arts." I used to think that this couldn't be popular since it is so violent. I am unfortunately mistaken. The ego-based person, who sees us as separate, is quite enthralled by this demonstration. The ego is fed by this demonstration of violent behavior; whether it is ours or someone else's, is not relevant.

Violence, competition for "stuff," seclusion, isolationism, are all methods that fear based people use to keep the ego fed or "safe."

Spirit "real" World

The spirit based person looks at people from the inside out. They see their brother or sister in source-spirit, and they recognize each other because they have their "spirit-glasses" on. They see the other for the joyful connection that they are and this brings a smile to their face.

Allow me to bring back Wayne Dyers concept of viewing people with special lenses, which view only the spirit of people. His description is so beautiful:

> *What you notice is pure love vibrating before*
> *your eyes… You see enormous strands of peaceful*
> *glimmering energy connecting each of us*
> Wayne Dyer
> *Being in Balance*

This is not a difficult task, if you can move your ego aside and realize, once and for all, that <u>we are the same.</u> Simply viewing people this way is a much more peaceful and relaxing way to see the world around us.

Citing Fr. Jim Koenigsfeld many years ago as he urged everyone in the congregation, while giving his sermon, to see each person they encounter as if that person were Jesus. It sure makes it easier to forgive the driver that just cut you off in traffic or the rude shopper that took the last item that you wanted off the shelf if you look at them as if they were actually Jesus.

The spiritual person understands that we are all trying the best we can, and the spirit is there if you just see beyond ego.

If you stop for a moment, right now and view the world, only as the spiritual, loving energy that emanates from the same source, you begin to see that everyone is a member of the same origin. To compete with one is actually to compete with the true self. Likewise, lifting others up has the effect of lifting ourselves up.

Those moved by spirit don't compete for material items in life. They *create* situations that manifest benefit for everyone's success, and joy. The person motivated by spirit understands that whatever is good for you is also good me. They give tirelessly of their time, and love.

Dharma' is that invincible power of nature which upholds
existence. It maintains evolution and forms the very
basis of cosmic life. It supports all that is helpful for
evolution and discourages all that is opposed to it
Maharishi Mahesh Yogi
Bhagavad-Gita

In the above passage, the Maharishi is referring to evolution in the spiritual sense, not as in survival of the fittest as coined by Charles Darwin, and used today to justify the reasons so many people are content with hurting others as a means of getting ahead, which is a manifestation of the ego.

The spiritual person sees giving is not out of a sense of obligation, for obligation does not resonate with the spirit. They know that in giving we keep the flow of abundance moving.

Those who are motivated by spirit do so because they find a great joy in such simple concepts as unconditional kindness and love. They are deeply moved by generosity in both giving and receiving. Once they have experienced this great joy they act in ways to generate more of it. Can there ever be enough true joy?

These people don't stand out in a crowd with the exception that they will go out of their way to come to the aid of another, without fear of reprisal nor seeking of recognition. They recognize the spirit in even the most fearful, angry person and seek to reach out to that spirit in the knowledge that angry, fearful people seek only forgiveness and to know that they are truly loved.

For where the spirit resides and is recognized, fear, anger, and hatred must cease to exist. In it's purest form, spirit prevails.

Love is the only response that undoes fear... Love any person
or situation that evokes fear in you and the fear will disappear
Paul Ferrini
Love Without Conditions

In Power Vs. Force, David Hawkins points out that force pales in comparison to power. Power is motivated by the spirit where Force is motivated by the ego...which one of those would you rather be a part of?

<u>Turning Point</u>

The turning point between spirit and ego in human interactions must be to peace and that understanding peace always comes from spirit and always is found within.

Wayne Dyer points out in his book, <u>Power of Intention</u>, that the giver, receiver and even an observer of any act of kindness are benefitted emotionally and even biochemically with increases of serotonin levels in their body.

Serotonin is a neurotransmitter that has many functions. In this case, it is used to enhance mood. Appropriate or elevated levels of this biochemical have the effect of putting people in a state of well-being.

It is more than simply a chemical response. Perhaps the biochemical response is triggered because there was a connection to Being. It is my belief that deep down we realize that we are furthering the evolution of the spirit as a whole every time we perform a simple act of kindness. Service to others brings us closer to source, It brings us closer to the meaning of the Sanskrit word, Dharma; that is, the purpose of our existence.

One way to make this connection is by giving. Give time, effort, and, yes, money. Don't be afraid that you will "run out." The law of abundance is clear about this. In giving you keep the flow of abundance moving. The bible is clear about this as well.

> *Give, and you will receive. Your gift will return to you*
> *in full--pressed down, shaken together to make room*
> *for more, running over, and poured into your lap...*
> *Luke 6:38*

Offer kindness to strangers. Today make a decision that you will offer kindness, whenever possible, anonymously, to a stranger. It can be a homeless person. Many people will not give to homeless people on a street corner because they believe that the person receiving will simply use the money for drugs, alcohol or cigarettes. Don't let this stop you. It is in the act of giving that the connection is enhanced. However, if you feel as though this is the case, you can give a jacket or blankets instead. Give to a church, or charitable organization. There are so many opportunities, on a daily basis, to give if we just look for them.

Often, when I get a cup of coffee at a drive up coffee shop, I will pay with a five-dollar bill. I pay for the coffee with the first two dollars, tip the barista a dollar and ask them to use the remaining two dollars for the next person who comes along. The first time I do it, they give me a perplexed look, and then I ask them if they have seen the great movie <u>Pay it Forward</u>? It is at this point that the act becomes clear. In doing something this simple, there is great impact. I feel better for giving, the barista will understand the impact of what I am doing and many times, are deeply affected by this act. Of course, the recipient of the anonymous gift will often feel moved. There have been places where I have started this and the next day the barista has told me that they started a Pay-It-Forward cup with the money and it actually GREW during the day. Because of this, I am moved to perform this simple act on a regular basis. This is just one simple example.

There are innumerable ways that you can have an impact on the lives of others by the simplest of acts. Hold a door for a stranger; let someone in your lane while driving. The other day I was in line to purchase something. The person in front of me did not have quite enough money for his purchase. I put the remainder of his tab on to my bill. He seemed deeply touched. I simply told him to pay it forward. To which he smiled and agreed.

Acts of kindness do not need to be enormous, philanthropic gestures. In fact, the ego rather than the spirit often motivates the large, highly visible acts of apparent kindness. Start simple. There are opportunities everywhere: A person sitting in a broken-down car on the side of the road is a magnificent opportunity to change someone's life. There are opportunities to do things anonymously as well, such as the pay-it-forward coffee cup.

Of course there are larger opportunities. As a teacher I am in a unique position to place a value on these types of acts and emphasize their value to my students. One such opportunity is having my classes anonymously sponsor a needy family for Christmas. When we do this we collect nonperishable food, money, presents and the holiday meal itself. Then we go over to the house when the family is away. We decorate, bring in food, and leave a card. My students have commented about this event after participating in it years after graduating. It had an impact on their life. There is no doubt that this was a turning point for them.

These opportunities are everywhere, if you just look for them. Be prepared when situations arise in which you can make a difference in a person's life. Find ways to touch another spirit, and help them feel safer, or stronger, or more confident. This can sometimes be as simple as using some kind words. Don't let it pass you by. Gratitude is always the by-product. The shear act of kindness toward another is self-perpetuating, and always touches the spirit.

Once you start doing small things for people and you receive the shear joy of the act itself, you will find yourself looking for opportunities to do it again. You will begin to note that the joy is infectious. <u>Let's all get that infection.</u> Remember...

You are a piece of God
Wayne Dyer
Power of Intention

If the previous statement is true, then so is everyone else. No matter how a person may drive their life, or what fears may fill them, they are a part of God, or Allah, or Buddha, or Being, or whatever name the loving, originating source energy may go by.

If we are all a part of the same source, then we are best served by serving each other. In service to each other, we are in service to God.

> *What we do to serve life automatically benefits all of us because we are all included in that which is life. We are life. It's a scientific fact that "what is good for you is good for me. <u>Simple kindness to one's self and all that lives is the most powerful transformational force of all</u>*
> David Hawkins
> Power Versus Force

The most powerful transformational force of all!!!!! What an amazing statement! This is not some abstract thought based on a few anecdotal records. Dr. Hawkins has drawn this conclusion from over three decades of research and testing using thousands of test cases. All of his findings are highly scrutinized and quantifiable. Here is yet another source of evidence regarding the way that we interact on a spiritual level.

> *Compassion and love are not mere luxuries. As the source of both inner and outer peace, they are <u>fundamental to the continued survival of our species.</u>*
> Dalai Lama

These are things that are "fundamental to the survival of our species." Let that sit inside you for a moment. Incredulous? Perhaps. What is the alternative: hate, fear, anger, competition? As yet another doomsday prediction draws near, due to the ending of the

Mayan calendar, it seems clear that the way to survive is through compassion and love. We can try to climb atop others or we can raise each other up.

Clearly love is the greatest power in the universe. As for me, I choose to interact through this. How about you?

Finally, follow the advice in a book entitled, <u>The Four Agreements,</u> by Don Miguel Ruiz.

1. *Be impeccable with your word:*
This means to be aware of the way that you speak to people. It is not only the intention but the words themselves can have an impact on the receiver, so choose them well.

2. *Don't take anything personally:*
Learn not to receive statements or actions from the others, especially those in an ego-state, personally. Simply listen to the message and be present to it.

3. *Don't make assumptions*
When people say or do things, don't assume that they had a particular motivation. This involves judging them, and that almost never has a happy outcome.

4. *Always do your best*
I love this message because it applies to so many situations. If you can always walk away from a situation feeling like you gave your best at that moment, not necessarily that it was 100 percent, because sometimes you just don't have 100 percent every day, but that you gave what you had at that moment, then feel good about the circumstances. They will more often than not turn toward spirit.

Jesus Life was all about service. He served mankind in the way that he taught, and interacted. His lesson of services is clearly illustrated in John 13:1-17, when he washed his disciples feet before the Passover. He preformed this Jewish ritual knowing that he would soon be crucified. He did this despite the behest of his disciples that it was they who should wash his feet.

Jesus ultimately served all of mankind by sacrificing himself. This is the ultimate Dharma… Service to life by the son of man

Peace And Harmony Or Anger Conflict And War

Peace and friendship with all mankind is our wisest
policy, and I wish we may be permitted to pursue it
Thomas Jefferson

THIS TOPIC TAKES HUMAN interaction into a more specific arena to discuss peace and war as it relates to human interaction. The reality is that this is still about human interaction, but deals with loss of life on global scales and fear that can be so forceful that all compassion is set aside, in the name of a flag or a cause.

I grew up in a time in American history, which was earmarked by the desire for peace. I am not talking about the stereotypical "peace man" which is so often depicted as the hippy, and I am not referring to just a trendy peace sign flashed as a style statement. Rather, I am describing a genuine peace in the world and brotherhood amongst all.

A great many men and women of the world lost their lives in the Viet Nam era. An exhaustive Internet search arrives at as many as 5.4 million men, women and children on both sides, directly and indirectly died as a result of this "conflict." The resulting feeling was a sense in many people that if we don't find peaceful solutions to our differences that it certainly leads to dire consequences. It is not my desire to enter into a political discussion. This is a general concern about how we seem to be approaching the solution to differences among nations and each other.

While the United States has the most forceful military on the planet, does that mean that we must use it so freely? Are there not more proactive ways to handle our differences?

I have noticed, among many people and on many cars, that the United States flag has been used more like a propaganda symbol in order to rally Americans behind actions that would not normally be acceptable. It is a shield used to supplant civil liberties and judge everyone. Many people see it as a vehicle to impose our will on the rest of the world. In school, the person that would beat up other kids on the playground just because they could was called a bully. The bully would pick on smaller kids and use intimidation as a means of gaining respect, or taking things for themselves.

So often we are informed, "We have been disrespected by this country or that dictator, or that our lives and freedom is somehow in peril." Patriotism becomes a battle cry, and those that do not wish to go to war are deemed as hating their country.

> *But I tell you who hear me: Love your enemies,*
> *do good to those who hate you, bless those who*
> *curse you, pray for those who mistreat you*
> Luke 6:27-28

This biblical edict was credited to Jesus of Nazareth. Today he would be labeled as anti-patriotic and maybe even a terrorist for this revolutionary teaching. Imagine that... Christian religions revere Jesus as the model that all should emulate, and yet he would be considered subversive for his views of peace and love.

Of course there have been people completely driven by a demented ego whose desire seemed to be the total control of the globe. Their fear was so massive that the only way to feel in control was to become a spiritual monster.

To stand against injustice, especially when it results in torture and death in masses, is not only appropriate but is a spiritual obligation. There are many examples of this, such as Adolf Hitler, Joseph Stalin, who is credited with the genocide of over 20 million in 23 years, Mao Tse-Tung. These fearful people achieved their positions of prominence through eliciting more fear and used fear to cause the deaths of so many.

Unfortunately there are also others that have translated patriotism into the, "We kick ass" mentality. Do people really feel that this is the best way to handle foreign affairs or is this fear position? Again, this sounds like the playground bully imposing his will, because he is stronger.

War for political, or monetary gains, or to prove a point is not acceptable. As beings of light, however we have a responsibility to come to the aid of the helpless and oppressed. Before violence is used, all forms of peaceful venues must be used first.

Author, Gerald Jampolski makes it clear in his book, <u>Love Is Letting Go Of Fear</u>, that there are only two human emotions: love and fear. He indicates that ALL other emotions are derived from this.

Love, of course is a manifestation of spirit, and fear, is that of ego. Further he clearly points out that people who lash out and attack others do so from a position of fear. This is supported in psychology journals, as evidenced in this passage:

> *As powerful as some bullies and criminals may*
> *be, just like the common or regular bully and*
> *criminal they fear the light and exposure*
> *Psychological Harassment Information Association*

All a person needs to do is look at the word that has become, perhaps the greatest leveraging term to instigate policies that fly in the face of human rights and freedom: Terrorist!

Terrorism has become a trigger-term in sustaining unorthodox methods of force and abuse of civil rights. It seems that any type of policy or "minor" human right violation are glossed over as long as it is in the name of Homeland Security against the terrorists.

What word could we use, that would conjure up more fear than this? If this generates terror in a person's heart simply by the image conjured from the word, then those wishing to illicit terror have already accomplished what they set out to do.

America will never be destroyed from the outside. If we falter,
and lose our freedoms, it will be because we destroyed ourselves.
Abraham Lincoln

There is a bumper sticker prevalently displayed on many US vehicles that states:

God Bless America

There is nothing about blessing others, or the whole world. Only bless America. All this does is promote separation, illicit fear, and perpetuate an us-against-the-world approach.

Yet those people who find themselves morally conflicted with the idea of war under the title of patriotism are labeled unpatriotic and anti-American. A brief review of American history shows us that some of the greatest Americans in history were at one time or another labeled as subversive or at the least, nonconformist. The continental congress that drafted the Declaration of Independence in 1776 comes to mind.

Isn't being a freethinking human and speaking your mind part of being free? I support the safety of ALL troops that go to war. I do not support war, unless it comes to the aide of the oppressed. Does that mean that I do not care for the country in which I live? Some would rationalize this.

Ego "real" World

> *Make the lie big, make it simple, keep saying*
> *it, and eventually they will believe it.*
> *Adolf Hitler*

The person lead by their egos may find that the answer to international pressures is to simply force our beliefs on others, or to take what we want because we can. It is their contention that we are right and the "other guy" is wrong. It is our responsibility to show them that. They believe that peace is having a bigger stick than the other guy. One of their biggest concerns is to elect a pacifist to the office of the presidency and that they will then dismantle our military leaving us "vulnerable" to attack. They have been conditioned to believe this. Look at the quote by Adolf Hitler again.

The ego driven person sees patriotism as more important than fellowship. They are willing to go to war to prove a point to the "bad" guys. Even if they are not clear on what the point is, or they have been told what to believe, such as another country having and preparing to use weapons of mass destruction. Nothing better than a strong dose of fear to make everything fair game.

> *What good is nationalism, what good is*
> *patriotism, if it destroys life itself?*
> *Michael Bernard Beckwith*
> *The Answer is You*

The only thing that matters to the ego-centered person is that we win. They watch news updates on war like it was their favorite sports team and they are watching game highlights.

When having a conversation with a friend a few years ago about why they were voting a particular way, they equated their vote with a vote against terrorism and that the "other guy" would let us be over-run by terrorists. Once again, we see fear and ego go hand-in-hand on a regular basis, as a means to control the masses

What are the things that we go to war over: fear of loss, such as loss of land, property, freedom, dignity, and religion, fear of death. Ego based people use euphemisms like "preemptive strike, or collateral damage" to justify countless deaths.

The very word terrorism has its roots in fear. It is derived from the Latin word *terrorem*, which means great fear or dread.

What is the egos response to fear? Attack or seclusion; these are the only two responses to fear on a global basis.

Most fear is first half of life formed and is dualistic in its nature. Richard Rohr is a Franciscan priest. In his CD on the <u>Two Halves of Life,</u> he discusses how people in the first half of their lives behave in a very dualistic manner. According to Rohr when people see dualistically they see things as black and white, good or bad.

A person in a dualistic mindset sees good guys and bad guys. They believe if we just kill the bad guys, everything will be all right. There are people that feel this is the best way to approach life. This is as ego-centered of an existence as there is. People thinking this way have made the judgment that their perspective is good and the other guy is bad. This is a separatist, ego-centered point of view.

<u>Spirit "real" World</u>

> *Non-violence is the greatest force at the disposal of mankind.*
> *It is mightier than the mightiest weapon of destruction devised*
> *by the ingenuity of man. Destruction is not the law of the*
> *humans. Man lives freely by his readiness to die, if need*
> *be, at the hands of his brother, never by killing him. Every*
> *murder or other injury, no matter for what cause, committed*
> *or inflicted on another is a crime against humanity*
> *Mohandas Karamchand Gandhi*
> *All Men Are Brothers*

Please re-read that passage. What a beautiful observation, from an amazing spirit... A spirit that comes from the same source as we do!

Most people would say that if anyone had a "right" to retaliate, it was Gandhi. He and his countrymen were beaten by British armies despite the fact that Gandhi and his followers were passive. If the information in the quote by Gandhi was available to him then it is available to us as well because we all come from the same source. Therefore we are able to access the same information as Gandhi. Mohandas Gandhi developed the concept of <u>Ahimsa, or the Way of nonviolence.</u>

First and foremost the spiritual person understands that we are all one. That we have the same source and that the real Being is there. There is no good or bad. There is no judgment. And that God should bless everyone unconditionally, because we do, and everyone is connected to the same common source.

There is only the spirit in a physical manifestation, learning lessons as they go along. They see our physical existence as temporary. Because they understand this, they realize that war can never serve the true being. Fear of land loss, or money or terrorism, is solely the possession of the ego.

While the spirit is not lost when the body dies, the spiritually centered person sees there is a great deal of damage to our soul when we take another life. Standing up for the innocent is not ego based... It is the realization that life... ALL life is sacred.

Spiritual people know that war for ego-centered patriotism, monetary or a political rationale never resonates at high frequencies of spirit or thought, and doesn't have desirable outcomes for anyone involved.

> *There never was a good war or a bad peace*
> *Benjamin Franklin*

Spiritually centered humans see that there is no good or bad guy. If a person has done their work and has reached the second half of their life spiritually, they realize that we are all on the same journey, and everyone expresses some level of "good" and "bad" based on how these are defined in that culture. Every law in every culture is defined differently and enforced differently based on the mores of that culture. It is not up to us to judge if it is right or wrong unless innocent lives are threatened.

Those living in spirit also realize, not only that the true self is in spirit but that they are not separate from other spirits; that, in fact, we are all part of the same beautiful, loving, caring, non-judgmental source. Many people call this God, or Tao.

In understanding this, they realize that it is counter-productive to go to war against others as this has negative effect on us. They even understand that being offended by something another person does, makes no sense, as we are one.

Further, they understand that love and compassion are their "weapons" against the act of war. Wayne Dyer shares an experience he had listening to the Dalai Lama. He gained two specific insights that I think are very pertinent here:

> *1) Compassion is the most important essential of human life*
> *2) If we were all raised to meditate on compassion on*
> *a regular basis over the course of our entire lives, war*
> *and violence would become completely nonexistent*
> *Wayne Dyer, after listening to the Dalai Lama*
> *Excuses Be Gone*

Ponder that for a few minutes. If compassion were the centerpiece of our existence, there would be no war, no good, no bad, no right, no wrong. Is this so far-fetched? Is it any more far-fetched to think that we currently live in a society that sees life dualistically, and that people attack each other rather than forgive each other? Is it more far fetched to believe that the answer to our problems is to kill another? Is one more feasible than the alternative? To the spiritually centered person, the answer is clear.

Turning Point

> *There is no way to peace... peace is the way*
> *A.J. Muste*
> *Clergyman, social activist*

In David Hawkings book, Power Vs. Force, Hawkings demonstrates, scientifically that one person approaching life from a perspective of the spirit, can cancel out the impact of far more than one person with negative, ego energy. In the same way that peace and love prevailed in the 1960s, because people really believed in it, this general sense can return if enough people are moved by their spiritual existence.

So if people make a daily habit of viewing and meditating on the idea that the world is a beautiful, loving, caring, nurturing experience then we change the way we experience life on a daily basis and our impact on it... exponentially.

If we experience life in the present without guilt, fear and especially without judgment of others, and ourselves, I believe that we will reach a "critical mass" of positive energy that will sweep the majority of this planet up in its light.

This is already happening. Think about it. If ignorant, fear-based destruction of life were more powerful than spirit-based existence, then our world would have destroyed itself several times over by now. We can turn this world into a living and joyful, spiritual world. It starts with a belief in spirit... spirit for everyone.

> *A simple act of kindness is the only action required.*
> *Forgiveness, gratitude, genuine caring are the foundation*

> *from which we must act. In doing so we walk in spirit, and*
> *we walk in the same footsteps as and along side Jesus Christ*

Avoid the "news." Very few stimuli are as toxic as the "news."… Remember that news is designed to be profitable. As such it uses sensationalism, which is so often fear-based, to sell. You are exposed to the smallest detail about every negative, egocentric event on the planet but rarely do you hear about the peaceful existence of the majority of our planet.

I truly believe that most of this world is filled with positive people but because fear sells, we have the minute percentage of the actions of other fear-based people placed in front of us constantly. I submit that there is a vast disconnect between the "news" and the majority of the world.

Look deeper. When you do hear the "bad" news, look into what is being said, who is saying it, and what their motivations are. Do not accept the statements at face value. Very often, someone may benefit from the control of other people by the fear elicited from the negative event, or "news."

See the world as loving and connected to each other. Meditate on this thought and realize that everyone in the world is doing the best they can. Be prepared to forgive them, on a large scale, when they make a mistake.

View war for what it really is: The taking of lives on a massive scale due to fear and ego-centrism. Use these simple criteria after you have looked deeper: Is this in defense of innocence or is this in support of fear?

Before you jump on the patriotism platform, try to use some empathy when looking at world issues. Realize that each culture is different and has had a different framework than the one that you have had. Think how different your neighbor is compared to you. How much more different will another culture be? Remember that just because it is not something you would do, does not make it wrong or right.

Support and perpetuate kindness and love to everyone that you meet, regardless of their behavior directed at you. The old saying "kill them with kindness," should be adjusted here to say, "Enliven them with kindness."

Worry And Regret Or Presence

I need neither future nor past, but to
learn to take today not too fast.
Jeb Dickerson

HONESTLY ASK YOURSELF, HOW often you worry about things that have not occurred; how often do you look back with regrets? In this world, we tend to keep our focus on things that have not occurred yet and hence fret about the future, or on things that took place in the past and carry with them, regret.

The word, future, from the Latin, *futura*, means going to be or yet to be, so they are not real. This often brings people to panic about incidents that have not happened. I believe that this is the nature of panic attacks. This is the so-called, "What if..." syndrome. What if she gets mad, What if I fall, What if the wheel comes off, What if the market crashes, What if someone knows what I am thinking? This goes on incessantly in our ego-minds.

When we focus on the future and worry about outcomes of things yet to come, or possible disasters, unfortunately we tend to attract negative outcomes. At the very least we add stress to our bodies and cause harm to our spiritual energy.

75% of the general population experiences
at least some stress every two weeks.
National Health Interview Survey (2009)
Stressfullives.com

Since the future is yet to come, we have the choice to be detached from the outcomes or base our happiness on them. If a person is dependent on outcomes in order to feel happy or sad, they are forgetting their true nature.

On a daily basis we are inundated with grim predictions of the future: someone breaking into your home, the downfall of market "futures," the housing future, the impending "end of the world future." We see it in the news, in commercials for companies that are trying to sell you things that will protect your future. We are also exposed to promises of prosperous futures.

If we just buy this product or have this cosmetic surgery or take this pill, our future will be bright. As kids we waited with great expectation for the future like Christmas, Thanks Giving, for the day that we would be old enough to do things that "adults" could do. This was anticipated with great excitement.

As we grow older, we are often taught to dread the future, because our bodies will get weaker, we will have great financial debts, our job responsibilities get greater, and the myriad of things that we are shown to fear in the "future." This is based on the people that are already in the "future" and we interpret their lives as something unpleasant and something that is inevitable for us.

In all situations, if we attach the way we will feel to
the outcomes of the future, we lack presence.

On the other hand, past, often viewed with regret, which means to remember with distress or longing, is a futile process that we have been taught to participate in over time. We see scenes of regret in our minds as they play over and over. Instead of the "What if" syndrome, this is the "If only" syndrome. If only I had not said that, If only I had answered differently, If only I had left, If only I had stayed, If only I had tried harder. Do any of these sound familiar?

As children we are taught by the use of "learning lessons," sometimes painfully and, over time, we learn to associate pain with the remembrance of certain events. These memories shape the way that we view the world for the rest of our lives. We respond to events that occur ten, twenty, and even fifty years later, based on the way we felt when we were eight years old, even though this is an inappropriate position of response.

We look back at events and feel as though we wish we could have done something different and regret the way that we treated people or circumstances or choices that we made. This leads to false emotional guilt.

Guilt is simply a hologram that brings pain and
destruction to our body, mind, and soul.

Still others look back in time and long for the "Good Ole' Days." This, nostalgia takes their minds away from the present and they cannot bring joy to their present. They have the inability to bring focus to making today better, and being present to the people in their lives, at this moment in time.

There is nothing un-spiritual in looking back with fondness but, as with attaching your happiness to the future, attaching it to the past does not allow present joy.

Ego "real" World

Those that view the world from the separatist ego-based perspective are obsessed with the past and future. Their awareness is so completely on those paradigms that they have little to no ability to be present to those around them or even themselves. It is impossible for them to meditate because they are always thinking about past events or what the future challenge will be. The only time that they have the ability to be present is in extreme situations, such as car accidents, or job loss, or the loss of loved ones, or an exhilarating ski run, or mountain bike ride. Outside of these types of situations they cannot focus on the present.

They have difficult times, listening to others without changing topics or adding their opinion. Their focus is so ego-based that they feel as if no one could have experienced as difficult a situation in their lives or faced the insurmountable obstacles that life continually throws at them. They also believe that their past experiences are far more important as are their ideas for the future, which is why they cannot listen to others very well.

This trait makes them extremely judgmental of others and situations, because nothing could have been or is going to be as bad or as good for someone else as it was or will be for them. This, in turn, leads them to a lack of trust in others.

They may often jump from one topic to another and lack sincere focus in conversations. They may be looking directly at someone as if listening intently but are already thinking about what they want to say in retort.

In fearing the present, ego-centered people find ways to bring focus to either future success or doom, OR they bring the focus to past regret or nostalgia.

In past years, we used to call these the non-stop coffee achievers or we classify someone as lost in the past. For many, the focus on future dread may lead to panic attacks or worse.

Some may bring so much stress into their lives that they make themselves physically ill over future concerns or past mistakes. Physical stresses based on past or future can lead to ulcers, and other intestinal disease. They may cause muscular trauma, which leads to structural issues. Those who live in regret or worry can do severe damage to their physical body.

Those living in past or future ego are always on the go. They have little if any ability to sit still and savor the moment. They see no purpose in wasting time looking at sunsets. They always need to be seeing what else is going on. They constantly see the grass as greener on the other side.

That being said, they also struggle with change. There is an innate inability to adapt to change from the outside, in their lifestyle. They have a severe lack of spontaneity, and become very flustered when their routine is changed. This, again, leads to more stress.

Spirit "real" World

Those living completely in spirit have the ability to live and love entirely in the moment. They are joyful in simply being present to someone or somewhere and can easily go with the flow. They have the ability to let go of the past and not judge people or events in any way but to simply "allow" the lesson that comes with every Universal experience.

> *We cannot take action in the past or the future.*
> *Past and future are born in the imagination*
> Deepak Chopra
> *The Seven Spiritual Laws of Success*

Those lead spiritually put their faith completely in a higher intelligence. This is the type of intelligence that orchestrates the interactions of billions of galaxies right down to caring for each individual. While they make plans, they also leave the details up to the universe, and enjoy the ride. They rarely become attached to possessions or outcomes.

In doing so, they have the ability to surrender to the moment. They may be in joy, or pain. They simply surrender to it with the understanding that it will lead to something beautiful.

They look constantly for the lesson and seek ways to serve others in Dharma. They seek their purpose and a means to express it, in service, to all those around them on a constant basis. They have learned to let go of past events, while learning from them.

They tend to be very trusting individuals. Because of this trust they tend to attract other people with the same focus. These are the people, in life, that listen intently to what you have to say and are always the people, in our lives, that we go to for help, compassion, and understanding.

Theirs is a world of constant giving because they know that all we have is this moment in time; possession of "stuff" is an illusion. They receive joy in the moment in reaching out to others in the "now" and have the ability to emanate that joy to those around them.

Turning Point

> *Yesterday is history. Tomorrow is a mystery. Today*
> *is a gift. That's why it's called a present*
> *Babatunde Olatunji*
> *Musician, Social activist, Educator*

This really says it all when it comes to the purpose of being present. It is a gift. This sounds very beautiful but how do we get to this place. In our current environment this is very difficult to completely shift to. Todays culture really does not let up when it comes to focusing on past and future but it is something that we can all strive for, and in doing so, we bring, into focus all that really matters.

To lead lives that are more present-focused, we need to learn to let go and seek inner present consciousness. There are many ways to let go.

Breathe.

When situations upset you, take a deep breath and let it go. Breathing is a powerful tool to help us be present. Breathing is a form of pure meditation and immediate presence. Try it now. Close your eyes and use your minds eye to see the collective molecules of air as they enter your body through the nasal passage, and down into your body's lung tissue. Notice as they rest in your lungs for a moment then are transformed and flow back up your air passage and out of your nose. Do this repeatedly, slowly, and use total awareness. In doing so you are completely present. No matter what situation you are in, or how stressful the situation may be, this is a simple way to bring yourself to presence.

Be present to your true body.

Feel your own "body." In this I am not referring to the physical body but rather the inner body of life. This is your consciousness. It is your connection to everything including source energy.

> *In your natural state of connectedness with Being, this deeper reality can be felt every moment as the invisible inner body, the animating presence within you... Underneath your outer form, you are connected with something so vast, so immeasurable and sacred that it cannot be spoken of-yet I am speaking of it now.*
> *Eckhart Tolle'*
> *The Power of Now*

What Tolle' is referring to is the reclamation of our own consciousness so that we may be present to the true self. He implores people to "feel" the inner body, to be aware of the life force within. This is the life force that gives life to the outer body and that is connected to all and to source. Again, close your eyes and visualize this life force as a warm and luminescent energy that is the real "you."

The deepest source of real power lies in consciousness

and the ability to be present in all circumstances
The Enneagram Institute
Understanding the Enneagram

Surrender.

Surrender to the moment. Like others whose bodies have aged, my physical body has taken on the resulting stresses of my own concern about the future and regret about the past. There have been times when I was completely incapacitated. I have grown to be grateful for this, because it is this physical pain that has launched me forward into seeking spiritual awareness to deal with these issues. The most important lesson I have learned, regarding my physical pain, is to be present and to surrender, in order to grow to my true Dharma. This awareness and ability to surrender to the physical pain and what it is teaching me has offered a type of body-meditation. It has allowed me to be more present to my body temple and to be grateful.

If you find your life situation unsatisfactory or even intolerable,
it is only by surrendering first that you can break the
unconscious resistance pattern that perpetuates that situation...
But in the surrender state a totally different energy,
a different quality flows into your doing. Surrender
reconnects you with the source-energy of Being
Eckhart Tolle'
The Power of Now

Serve. Find your Dharma

Do your best to view life without worry or regret. These ego-thoughts can only cause damage to our true purpose. We are here to discover our Dharma and serve others. How can we do that if our minds are focused on regret, nostalgia, anticipation or worry? There is no presence in this thinking. Presence is the only way to truly know self.

> *The seventh spiritual law, the law of Dharma or purpose*
> *in life, says that we are spiritual beings who have taken*
> *physical form to fulfill a purpose… When we blend this*
> *unique talent with service to others we experience the ecstasy*
> *and exaltation of our spirit. This is the goal of all goals.*
> Deepak Chopra
> *The Seven Spiritual Laws of success*

Give some of your "stuff" away. Give money to the needy or help someone get back on their feet by giving your time and energy. The key here is to serve the universe by giving of the things that you think make you what you are. All material possessions are past or future-based. In the present you have nothing.

If you think that you are a well-dressed person, then give your clothes. If you feel that money, in some way, defines you, then give financially. If your life is working at a job, learn to give that time to those that have no job. In giving up the "stuff" in your life, you let go of the past and stop fretting about protecting your future. You allow yourself to simply be present in the moment and to "be."

Laugh.

Find ease in the moment. There is nothing more present than laughing. Deep, generous laughter is one of the truest ways to experience the nature of the spirit.

> *Laughter is the nectar that flows directly from the soul*
> Michael Bernard Beckwith
> *Spiritual Liberation*

Find things to laugh about in your life. Every time that something goes "wrong" in your daily life, you have the choice to be the victim or to simply laugh. You may even laugh at your initial response of feeling victimized, and how silly that really is. What kinds of things am I talking about? These are events, large and small: You slip and fall, walk into a door, or spill something, instead of adding the negativity of feeling like a victim and becoming angry, try to catch yourself and change the emotion to laughter. Locate it deep inside and enjoy it.

Let others around you even wonder about your laughter to the point of thinking that you might be a little off your rocker. What more fun could you have? By laughing we not only see the humor in every day situations, we immediately realize the truth about the real world, and that the physical, ego, past and future world is the real illusion. Laughing is the ultimate self- awareness, and the ultimate in presence.

Be with nature.

Try to experience nature whenever possible. Go out into nature and simply experience life in its purest form. Don't think about it or try to analyze it…just be present in that moment. Be alone, and quiet. Sit and observe without judgment. Feel the preciousness of the moment that you are in. Nature is a true miracle on a moment-to-moment basis, yet we take it for granted. It becomes the trees that we pass by on the highway in our cars on the way to work. Every time that I have participated in being present to nature, and become a part of it, I have felt the tranquility that it provides. It may be the closest we can get to God in purest form. Sit and enjoy the mountains or the sunset over an ocean horizon. Your worries and regrets will fade away.

Go with the flow.

Adopt an attitude of going with the flow and learn to be grateful for this moment.

> *Whether or not it is clear to you, no doubt*
> *the universe is unfolding as it should*
> *Max Ehrmann*
> *Desiderata*

One afternoon, try going out somewhere with no plans but simply say "yes" to whatever opportunity presents itself. No matter how difficult it may be, simply say yes. It doesn't matter what it is. The source of all will not put you in peril or ask you to do something that is not appropriate for all.

> *Those who hope in the Lord will renew their strength*
> *They will soar on wings like eagles; they will run and*
> *not grow weary they will walk and not be faint*
> *Isaiah 40:31*

To be present we must trust in the present moment, with good reason. There are no failures in the present. There are no obstacles in the present. There is only the now. It is here for a reason, and if we are grateful for it, we can grow and move more to spirit. That is a pretty good reason.

Remain present to those around you, to the gifts of each moment. Stay vigilant and look for lessons to learn and to discover your own gift. This is the gift that you will share for the betterment of all… There is no greater present.

Perhaps the greatest lesson of all is simply to enjoy this moment, because it is all you really have.

> *You are not a human <u>doing</u>, you are not a human <u>was</u>, and*
> *you are not a human <u>will be</u>… You are a human <u>being</u>*

Responsibility

If you could kick the person in the pants responsible for
most of your trouble, you wouldn't sit for a month
Theodore Roosevelt

RECENTLY IT WAS THE fifteen-year anniversary of a very famous lawsuit in which a woman was awarded over two million dollars for getting burned by a coffee that she purchased in a fast food restaurant. The suit was based on the coffee being too hot and that there was no statement on the cup which warned the consumer that the coffee was indeed, hot. This incident has become the poster-child for litigations of all types in the world. People sue for all types of reasons from falling on ice to walking into doors. No one seems willing to take responsibility for their own actions. Everyone, it seems, is looking for someone else to blame for their problems.

I watch very little television, but when I do, I notice that there is quite often commercials for drugs that advertise the salvation found in their particular drug. Every ailment from obesity to allergies, to depression to erectile dysfunction insomnia, and the list goes on. By law, the companies must list the side effects of their drug and the list is extensive. There is a particular drug that is taken to help in depression, in which one of the side effects is a suicidal tendency. That does not exactly sound like the type of trade-off that most people would be looking for in order to help them feel better.

What is it that both of these scenarios have in common? There is a significant lack of self-responsibility. These are just two cases where people take or are offered opportunities to remove responsibility for the circumstances in their lives. Responsibility is diverted or avoided all together rather than handling situations in a responsible manner, or finding the wherewithal to manage these circumstances within their own abilities.

Lawsuits are a perfect example. Now there are certainly legitimate reasons to pursue legal action when someone is truly injured due to a serious hazard and in which this is the only course of action that will correct the situation, but society and especially American society has become so litigious regarding every aspect of life that it is difficult to think of any situation that does not have the potential for legal action.

If a person slips on the sidewalk, they sue the city because there was too much dirt. Some one sues their boss for pain and suffering because they have to work too hard. So many seem to believe that it was not our fault and that someone else must be to blame. Adding fuel to this action, people seem to feel entitled to "their fair share" of another's pie through lawsuits.

The very act of taking a pill to deal with depression or even medical infirmities has become so commonplace that no one seems to think twice about it. The drug companies continue to make money hand over fist because people would rather take a pill than learn how to deal with the cause of illness. A pill can only deal with symptoms... There has never been a pill that can cure anything.

Yet people take them to mask symptoms rather than accept responsibility. They don't see that they have the ability to heal rather than continuing to cover up the effects of whatever imbalance their body may be experiencing

Now I do want to say that it is difficult to heal while we are in pain so there is a use in medication to allow people to seek out the cause of the symptoms. Unfortunately, we as a society tend to use the medication as the cure because we may feel better as a result of taking the pill, and then do not go deeper into healing.

These are examples in which we have allowed our existence to evolve without being responsible. There are numerous other examples. As previously referenced, this comes from the sense of entitlement. The only reason that this is present is because so many people still see themselves as individual. They think, "This is MY body. This is MY mind. These are MY thoughts."

I see these attitudes reflected in school among the students that I am blessed to teach on a daily basis. As a teacher I hear these words from my students all too often whenever they earn a poor grade: "You gave a bad grade on this." Rather than accepting responsibility for the work and trying to do better, they feel as though they are the victim and blame me for their grade. I often have to field questions from the parents about why I am picking on their child, rather than, what can they do to help their child do better in class. It is an endless cycle and will continue to be until everyone takes responsibility for himself or herself.

When I was a treatment counselor this was called being in the victim cycle. The victim cycle is prevalent today and takes conscious responsible, awareness to break.

Ego "real" World

The person driven by ego sees the world as owing them and therefore they take a victim posture when they are not given things. They have a sense of entitlement rather than being humble and accepting blessings with contrite hearts They are unable to see failure as an opportunity to learn a lesson and prefer to play the role of the victim. Their focus is about them. They do not see their role in the world as part of a contributing member.

On another level they see the world, dualistically, as good versus bad and if we just get rid of the "bad guys" then "us good guys" can be successful and happy. The responsibility for their happiness comes externally rather than being happy from the inside. They tend to have a materialistic view of happiness. They may see a lawsuit as a means to get rich from someone else's money.

They believe that they will find happiness in possessions. The possession of money, and not the effort that goes into making money will fulfill them. Gaining power without treating people in a way that garners respectful power will make them feel good. As students they see the grades and not the knowledge that leads to good grades. Dating physically attractive or wealthy people will complete their lives and not the growth and spirit that goes into building a strong mutual relationship. If they can just get that next great external pleasure they will finally be content.

No matter how many ways that they attempt to fulfill their own happiness through external pleasures, it remains just out of reach and always will because they never take responsibility for it themselves, and their happiness is not defined on the spiritual level.

Ego driven people tend to complain the most about how they have been wronged, and always seek a source of blame for what they see as problems. They look for the easy way to "fix" situations and never seek to self-evaluate. Nothing seems fair to them and do not see the point in charity or serving others.

Their problems are always someone else's fault. They will even blame God. They look for easy relief from ailments. The ego driven person turns quickly to medications that simply mask symptoms and do not allow healing while creating a myriad of other problems through side effects.

If there is a get rich quick plan or a magic pill out there, they will seek it.

Spiritual "real" World

Although the world is full of suffering,
it is also full of overcoming it
Helen Keller

Some of the happiest people in the world have taken total responsibility of their own lives and realize that everything that happens "to" them is simply an *opportunity to learn lessons and grow and to become more spiritually self-aware.*

They do not see "good" or "bad" events or situations in their lives, and they never blame others. There is only the next step toward their ultimate purpose. They feel truly blessed, on a daily basis, and are content from the inside out. Even in pain, even when they slip on a dirty floor or get scalded with hot coffee or have been stricken with a disease.

They know that depression is an opportunity to grow and learn more about themselves. That suffering is part of life's way of getting your attention. All too often we want someone to take away our suffering. Those who view life from a spiritual point of view have learned to merge with suffering and to acknowledge it is part of the healing process. They know that the pain is a part of them and is a vehicle to a greater level of awareness and existence. They do not look to blame others for it. Why would they blame others for this gift?

I myself have dealt with back and hip pain for a great many years. In my healing, I have turned to many spiritual teachings and it has taken me to a place that I never would have arrived at had I not reacted to my pain as a gift. It has been a gift that I would not go back in time and take away even if I could. I feel certain in saying that I never would have written this book had my physical pain not lead me to seek out spirituality.

If you are running a fever, instead of thinking, I

> *must be sick, think, my body is cleansing. These*
> *responses acknowledge your body's intelligence as*
> *well as taking responsibility for your health*
> Donald Epstein
> *The 12 Stages of Healing*

Epstein's statement illustrates two important points:
1. Rather than seeing symptoms of illness as being sick, see them as your body's way of healing.
2. Taking responsibility for your health rather than leaving it in the hands of a doctor or someone else.

Are there times of physical injury in which hospital care is a must? Certainly! But spiritually lead people do not seek out others to cure them of every ache and pain. Instead they surrender to the pain and seek out what it has to teach.

Those who move from the spirit see their happiness as their responsibility.

> *They know that happiness comes from growing and*
> *learning and self-realization in their spiritual journey,*
> *and that they are responsible for their own happiness.*

They are forgiving endlessly and often help to console others in pain. They know that their purpose is found in serving others and will go out of their way to do so. In doing so, they are further healed.

> *And the King shall answer and say unto them, Verily I*
> *say unto you, Inasmuch as ye have done it unto one of*
> *the least of these my brethren, ye have done it unto me*
> Jesus
> Matthew 24:50

Spiritual people understand that in service, not blame, we are served and the entire universe benefits from this.

At no time do spiritual people consider lawsuits over petty issues or look to blame the world for their pain or misfortune. Whenever these issues arise they see it merely as an opportunity to grow and to serve. They do not see "good" or "bad" occurrences. They do not judge what has happened. They only see all events as things that they have attracted to themselves and, as such, they are important in their ultimate growth towards their ultimate purpose. This leads to gratitude.

Turning Point

When a person realizes that they are a part of a greater whole. They see the "real world" is not so much the physical exterior that they see but the spiritual world that they become aware of by serving others with gratitude and they approach life with joy.

When people see others as "a piece of God," then there is no need to blame. We are all a part of the same unity and are striving together for all that comes from that. By helping each other we realize that we are helping the greater cause that includes ourselves.

By viewing pain as an opportunity to truly heal in a way that no pill can ever accomplish then we put that responsibility squarely where it belongs and we all become the better for it.

There are occasions when the body is in great pain and relief is required from an outside source, but to reach the spiritual plain, do not seek to use external forms of relief for every level or type of pain.

Pain is a gift. See it as a means to learn and that spirit is getting your attention. Pain is NOT God punishing you for something you did wrong. It simply is a tool to help you gain awareness of the self and go inside to seek answers. Surrender to it.

> *As you begin to take full responsibility for your life,*
> *circumstances lose their power over you and you activate the*
> *dimension of your soul character that yearns to express*
> Michael Bernard Beckwith
> *Spiritual Liberation*

So what does your authentic self, the real self, the self that is a common part of the whole source, <u>yearn</u> to express?

Through meditation and quiet time, we may find the answer to the previous question. If we pay attention and take responsibility for all that takes place in our lives, we will see what our Dharma is… we will know our true purpose in service.

Responsibility is more than "fessing" up when we have done something wrong; it is accepting that all things that happen "to" you actually come from within with purpose and all are opportunities to reach the truest potential you are as a being of source, peace, and joy. When you see these as gifts then you view them in a way that teaches you to look for how the gift may help you evolve forward.

> *However, life with its challenges stimulates*
> *our growth and development*
> Michael Bernard Beckwith
> *Spiritual Liberation*

Have you ever felt that there is a part of you that is trying to express itself, but only needs the opportunity to do so?

> *That opportunity is found in every one of life's challenges, for*
> *it is only when we are challenged that we must examine life*
> *within, and that is the time when we learn and grow the most*

Learn to enjoy those challenges, rather than looking for someone or something else to blame, because in learning and growing during those challenges, you will evolve into something even greater than before you started the journey. God is not punishing you.

God is offering you the opportunity to become more "you."

Consumption And Consumerism

Earth provides enough to satisfy every man's
need, but not every man's greed
Mohandas K. Gandhi,
Quoted in E.F. Schumacher, Small Is Beautiful

THE NEXT TIME THAT you are driving down a city street or watching television, or even listening to the radio, pay close attention to the amount of consumption that abounds. Much of our western world thrives on consuming goods as large and conspicuous as we can achieve.

This attitude is in large part a major contributor to the economic state that our society was thrust into starting in the later half of 2008. The belief that people had to own, bigger, more extravagant homes, cars, and more, lead to people borrowing more than they could or should to stay within their means. When the economy went south, these loans were called in and people could not settle up. There were1.4 million personal bankruptcies in 2009 according to creditcard.com.

A great many people seem to look to material goods or awards, recognition or other outward expressions of success to help them feel good. They long for something to quench their inside thirst; something to fill a void that they feel. These are pleasures that are superficial and do not last. They are never a substitute for the real happiness that comes from the knowledge of our real self.

All too often this void is fed ceaselessly with material items. But no amount of slow energy, material can ever satiate this void. Now more than ever, especially in the west, humans look to conspicuous consumption as a means to derive happiness. There are numerous examples that have surfaced in the last ten years.

There seems to be a cavalier sense of using, buying, owning, hoarding all that we can simply because the means to do so have been made available.

Is this not the very definition of the separatist ego world? This is the view that there is only so much stuff, and I need to take from you to get mine. Individuals define themselves by the "stuff" they have.

> *The average American house size has more than doubled*
> *since the 1950s; it now stands at 2,349 square feet.*
> *Whether it's a McMansion in a wealthy neighborhood,*
> *or a bigger, cheaper house in the exurbs, the move toward*
> *ever-larger homes has been accelerating for years*
> *Margot Adler*
> *Behind Ever-Expanding Dream House*
> *July 4, 2006*

In the same article, Ms. Adler identified the following growth pattern from National Association of Home Builders (see graphic "From Modest to McMansion"):

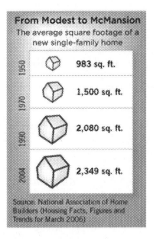

115

We seem to want to own the biggest cars and sport utility vehicles regardless of the damaging CO_2 released into the atmosphere (see chapter on environment). Many people drive massive vehicles that run 5-10 miles to the gallon, in spite of the common realization of how much pollution goes into our atmosphere. Big is never big enough. There is always something bigger and more massive. Trucks, SUVs and even a number of sedans increased in size and grossly ostentatious displays of consumption. This type of consumption has been used as the prototype for the American Dream.

In a world that seemed to have no limits, westerners used that as a rationale to legitimize destruction of wilderness and drill for oil in formerly pristine nationally preserved land. Rather than keeping their lavish living within reasonable limits, they have responded with a sense of entitlement to the detriment of wildlife, nature, as well as other countries. This is a recipe for disaster.

> *The United States consumes almost a third of the*
> *world resources with only about 5% of the world*
> *population. Almost 99% of consumer goods purchased*
> *end up in the trash inside of six months*
> *Anne Leonard*
> *The Story of Stuff*

Often we turn to credit cards when we do not have enough money to purchase the items that we believe will fill the bottomless pit inside us. We have been taught that if we cannot afford something, then just charge it. Credit card companies are making a fortune off of the interest that the average person pays by carrying balances.

> *Oh, for the good old days when people would stop*
> *Christmas shopping when they ran out of money*
> *Author Unknown*
> *Quote Garden*

2011 figures indicate that there are 609.8 million credit cards held by US Consumers and the average credit card debt, for those with debt, is 15, 799 dollars according to creditcards.com. We are taught by big business, that in order to be happy, you must have certain material items, and if you cannot afford them, then you should purchase them through credit. While there are a number of emergencies that arise, in my opinion, vast numbers of people continue to use credit as a means to fill a gaping hole deep inside that can not be sated by material substance. This hole is present because they have not seen the truth of who they really are.

In the last ten years, it has been my observation that kids are inundated with mp3 players, cell phones, portable games, and other such fun electronic devices, to the point that it has drastically changed the way that they interact even with each other. Rarely do people go for walks in nature or appreciate what they already have with the people in their lives.

As I look down the halls of the high schools in which I teach, I see student's texting other people whilst walking alongside their friends that they are not even interacting with. By trying to use these devices to be more social, they have lost the interpersonal skills to be present to the people around them. They find identity in the device and have near-pathological attachments to these items.

These items come to us at the cost of our natural resources, either by their manufacturing, use or their disposal. We have allowed our desire to have and hold superficial possessions to supersede the priority of caring for our surrounding, and even lose sight of it.

Somewhere along the line our society decided that nature was here to serve us rather than it be a source of respect. Humans seem to have decided that natural existence is somehow beneath an anthropogenic life. Through technology, we have increased the carrying capacity of this planet but the human population cannot be sustained in the extravagant manner in which it currently inhabits, particularly in the United States.

All too often we, and especially our children are more and more secluded from nature because we believe, and we pass this belief on to our children, that we will be fulfilled by the conspicuous consumption that currently represents our lives. As a result, we openly destroy more of these natural surroundings to fill the bottomless pit of pleasure desire.

We don't even see that this act will result in our own undoing.

We somehow have a belief that we can replace spiritual fulfillment with material pleasures at the expense of the world around us. Our craving for more has destroyed a vast amount of natural habitats through clear-cutting, deforestation, irresponsible mining, and the like.

A great many companies outsource their labor to other countries because labor laws and restrictions are so much lower than in the United States and everyone still wants the best price for their toys. This leads to continuous destruction of natural surroundings, land and resources.

Because of this destruction, the native people and wildlife that lived off of the natural resources in these areas, now have to leave the land and enter cities, keep searching for an ever-shrinking mass of natural resource, or die.

Ego "real" World

> *The tyranny of trends is blasted out at us from television, radio, newspapers, tabloids, computers and even our dentists waiting room, attempting to convince us that we must smell a certain way, wear a certain label, weigh a specific weight, have whiter teeth, drive a certain car, make a certain income, and so on, before we can consider that we've "made" it.*
> Michael Bernard Beckwith Spiritual Liberation

Those that live by ego, see the world as their oyster to take and use and consume. They see that the mere conspicuous consumption of materialistic items provides status to them and that is a status that they seek and feel will fulfill them.

"Enough" does not exist to them, and they are never happy with what they have. They buy a new car every year and still it does not satisfy the need for more. They own the latest electronic devices at the expense of the people in other countries, which are often young children, who work for pennies a day just to put food on the table.

They do not have real concern for stewardship or even leaving viable conditions for sustainable living here for younger generations as long as they "get theirs." They see nature as something to use or to hunt, or to exploit, or as an obstruction to clear out. Often the prevailing sentiment is not to be concerned about the current environment because it will not affect their lives for many years to come.

They think that they find happiness in the ipods, and computers, and cars, and houses, and even people that they own and display. They seek their joy in the material world and have little to no connection to nature that does not, in some way exploit it. They do not realize that they will never find true joy in the short-lived pleasures that they seek.

They may claim to be connected to God or to be religious but do not see God in all living things. They are completely caught up in the "tyranny of trends."

They cannot make the connection between their electronics or expensive cars, or unsustainable use of resources and their own relationship to the world and to source.

Spirit "real" World

I love to think of nature as an unlimited

> *broadcasting station, through which God speaks*
> *to us every hour, if we will only tune in*
> *George Washington Carver*
> *(Quote Garden)*

The spirit-based person needs so little slow-energy material to be happy. They own only the most basic items and find joy in that. They find happiness in simply being present and the joy of co-creating. Even in this technology-driven planet, simple things that bring them close to source satisfy them.

This is not to say that they do not own computers or ipods, or tablets... They just don't let those things own THEM! They can walk away from these things as easily as they attained them.

The spiritual person has a strong connection to the natural world. They spend regular time in nature or partaking in nature in the form of gardening, caring for their pets, relaxing in their yards. Simply being at peace and being present to nature brings them joy. They realize that the connection we have to nature is the connection that we have to our source, and spending time within it is a sanctuary of true worship in source energy.

A dear friend of mine is a self-professed atheist, but spends so much time in nature that he has gained a true love and connection to it. He may be one of the most spiritual people I know.

Those lead by the spiritual energy can be in nature without the need to take more than they need from it or disturb it. They simply are present to it, and enjoy the true connectedness that they have in it. They realize that their brothers and sisters: the trees, and birds, and animals all come from the same source and are filled with the same life that we all are. They feel the true sense of one-ness with that, which comes from source. If you walk with them, they can enjoy themselves having a quiet stroll and simply sharing space.

They seek and find true joy both outside, among other people and nature, as well as within, through meditation. They understand that recognizing the truth about ourselves, that we are spiritual in nature, is all they need to be filled with joy. They express this outwardly by serving others, and being present to all around them.

> *The Lives of Jesus, the Buddha, and holy people like St.*
> *Francis, St. Theresa, and Gandhi all reflect the belief*
> *that the path to spiritual union is one of relinquishment*
> *of material things. Jesus taught that a camel could go*
> *through the eye of a needle more easily than a rich man*
> *with many possessions can enter the kingdom of Heaven*
> Donald Epstein
> *The 12 Stages of Healing*

> *Those lead by spirit understand and live by the paradigm,*
> "Live simply, so that others may simply live."

Turning Point

So how do we get there? How do we learn to live simply and be content with that? Below is a series of steps that a person can take to learn how to recognize the spirit, that is already there, and whose joys are derived from being connected, not in being separate.

Escape the bombardment from the media that more is better or that fear is a reason to buy something.

On a daily basis we are bombarded with ads that sell the latest and greatest or use fear tactics to motivate you to purchase goods or services that protect you and your family… all of these motivations are designed to create more separation between you and the source connection that you have to all of creation. You need to remove the stimulus whenever possible. It is not an easy task. We are hit from TV ads, Internet, newspaper, billboards.

Make the conscience decision to renew your connection by turning away from these things whenever possible. Turn off the TV, power down the computer, and stop reading the graphic headlines. When you are exposed to these commercialisms, see them for what they are. Ask yourself if what you are exposed to is coming from spirit.

Connect with nature.

Spend time alone in nature. Take a leisurely stroll in the woods or in the mountains, or on a beach, even in a park. Go there without any motivation to do anything other than to simply be with it, listen to it, smell it, feel it. Let it fill you with the joy of the connection that you have with it, but may have denied, forgotten, or discarded. The more a person spends with the natural world, the more they realize that we are all a part of the same wonderful connectedness. There is great soul to be found in nature.

Connect with people.

To connect with someone is one of the most basic things that we can do to reaffirm that we have a common source and to celebrate that. Call a friend that you have not spoken to in a long time, make a lunch date, reach out.

This is not limited to people that we know. You can connect with someone by using a simple gesture like a smile, or a peaceful look at the grocery store. Strike up a conversation with the person that checks your groceries or sells you coffee. Go to a shelter and help feed the homeless. Don't just donate to help. Be there, physically. Give them your joyful presence. When you are there, you can truly connect. Connecting is such a simple thing and yet we tend to stay behind our walls even when we are actually in society. I have noticed, anecdotally, that it seems many older people have a glow to them. They seem to already see the connection between us all.

The more that you connect with people the more that you will feel at home, and you will walk away with a spiritual experience of joy.

Do things with your hands.

Something as simple as tending a vegetable garden, or raising flowers, can be greatly satisfying. It should be something that supports life as a general rule. All too often we tend to sit at computers or drive on long stretches of road and forget the joy of partaking in something that co-creates with life. Deep inside we all have the desire and inspiration to create, but it has been diluted by the egoic ideas that we are constantly bombarded by on a daily basis.

My father was so good at building things and worked in his workshop almost as a form of meditation. He maintained a garden and there was great joy in his eyes as his vegetables grew to bear fruit. The food that we received as a result of his raising it was so much more full of life than anything that can be bought at a store. It fed our spirit.

Spend time creating.

Speaking of creating, one of the greatest satisfactions that we can have as humans is to create something that is life affirming. Creating a painting, or sculpture, writing a book, helping to build a home for Habitat for Humanity, or create a snowman in the winter. Create a trail for other people to enjoy and connect with nature. What can affirm life and its connection more than the creation of something that comes from within?

Many people "feel" things subtly trying to rise to the surface. They often will see reminders in the physical world of the presence of the gift within. Sometimes it is as simple as a billboard that advertises painting classes, or writing classes, or guitar lessons. It doesn't matter what the gift is, it is up to us to act on it. Deep down, you know what it is. You are moved when you received gentle nudges. Sadly, many people will ignore the internal message. Eventually they ignore them so long that they will not be able to hear the small whispers of inspiration.

Remember these gifts are there for you to reconnect with the "real" world that is spirit.

In all things, BE PRESENT!

It is a cliché to say it anymore these days, but being present to the moment is critical and something that we so rarely do. No matter who we are with or what the situation we often tend to think about where we are going next or what happened the night before or even what we want to say to the person that we are talking to, rather than listening to them and being completely present to them.

Slow down, leave time, breathe and be present to people, to nature, to the wind, to yourself. We often try to cram in more tasks, daily, than we should. While we "accomplish" more, we lose the spirit of life. Do yourself a favor. Take your daily to-do list and cut it in half. Savor each moment that you have when you drive, walk, eat, and interact.

Your presence is the greatest gift that you give at each moment
of the day, far greater than any monetary object can ever be

Accept yourself.

You are perfect. I am referring to the "you" that is the spirit... the image of God... the true "you." True love can never be expressed by slow energy material. True love is self-accepting, self-love, self-surrender. Surrender to the inside and you will not need external items to fill the void.

Q: What is happiness?
A: Happiness is the state of being connected...of belonging.
When you are disconnected, you will inherently be unhappy
Richard Rohn
Franciscan Catholic Priest

He did not reply that you need the biggest car, the biggest house, the most toys, the best looks, spend money frivolously, or even have the biggest crucifix. He simply said that you need to be connected to all sisters and brothers of this world, and none of that requires any money or superficial pleasures.

This is not easy, as everywhere we go in public, we are inundated with music, computers, ipods, and cell phones. These things keep you connected to the physical world but take away from true connectedness in the spiritual world and with each other at a much deeper level. All of these things are slow-moving material distractions that take us away from connecting with each other on a daily basis. We must find opportunities to put these items down and to connect to those around you, whenever possible.

Today, more than ever, it seems that people look to material goods as their derivation of personal value and satisfaction. However, it is my hope and sense that there are more people that are seeing the truth about being connected to the "real" world, and not being connected to their possessions.

The happiest people live with less and less but realize the vital need and desire to stay attuned to the spiritual commonality that we are all a part of.

We all yearn to see who the real self is, the ghost in the machine. We all have a sense that it is not our mind or body; that there is something so much deeper.

Keep looking. Seek and never stop seeking to meet the connection to source. This is truly who we are. We are the selves without material, and without even flesh. This is the high-energy commodity that we have with each other and cannot be purchased with money.

Religion And A Spiritual Existence

What is God? The eternal One Life
underneath all the forms of life.
What is Love? To feel the presence of that One
Life deep within yourself and within all creatures.
To be it. Therefore all love is the love of God.
Eckhart Tolle'
The Power of Now

ANYTIME, EXISTENTIALISM IS THE topic, there will be a variety of opinions. Some are secular, some are orthodox religious, some are strictly about spirituality, many are somewhere in between. It may seem odd for a person who teaches high school chemistry to make observation and inference about religion and spirituality, but remember that I am human first and spend a great deal of time with my students.

An interesting aspect of teens is that they express their feelings openly, particularly about such a volatile topic as religion and spirituality. Additionally, being both a scientist and a teacher attunes my mind to various opinions without judging those opinions.

Human beliefs about God, Buddha, Krishna, Tao, on and on, can be as strong as the cosmic energy from the Sun and, being human, we defend our beliefs vehemently when we feel attacked. After all, our entire existence depends on it or so we may believe. We all arrive at a place in time based on our experiences and clouded by how those experiences affect our beliefs. So how do we look at our beliefs about existence?

Religion is a term based from the Latin word, *religionem*. Take a look at the following definitions of religion.

1) State of life bound by monastic (religious) vows
2) Conduct indicating a belief in a divine power
Online Etymology Dictionary

Some might say that religion is defined by the first definition, and spirituality by the second. Everyone has varying ideas of these concepts, but few would agree that religion and spirituality have the same meaning. There are about twenty or so recognized religions in the world, but no one would say that one type of spirituality is different than another.

Wars have been fought over religion, but I have never heard of a war being fought over spirituality. Many religions have their own set of rules that are set against the cultural norms and have caused a great amount of angst among the members of that culture.

There have been countless numbers of people, tortured, and executed in the name of a deity or belief. During the reformation, the Spanish inquisition, Muslim zealots and many others executing in the puritan beliefs of scripture. History is filled with examples of Christianization of "pagan" people while being over-run by "God-fearing" invaders. These "pagans" were given the ultimatum to convert or die. The human time-line is filled with atrocities in the name of religion or a deity. To this point and to the best of my awareness, these things have not occurred in the name of spirituality.

Maybe spirituality has some commonality to it. Let us delve into this concept from the perspectives of the ego and the spirit.

<u>Ego "real" World</u>

An ego based person sees God or any other supreme "being" as separate from them, as separate as they see other people, animals, and trees, etc. While they attend church, they often view it as a way to "be" with God for an hour.

They may hold strong to the thought that if they say the right words, process the correct rituals, sing the correct hymns then they are closer to God than other people.

These people may be fine upstanding, and happy citizens that you trust and are trust-worthy. They may give to charity, and always put money in the donation plate. Dare I say it, that in some way, deep in their minds, they may even feel that giving money is a way to buy their way to heaven. To them, heaven is a place up there and God is a stately old man keeping a scorecard of your "good" deeds and "bad" deeds. At the end of their lives, if you have more "good" deeds than "bad" ones, then they get to go to heaven.

> *They hold up the Bible as a cookbook to get to heaven. In some way, these people may even believe that God wrote the Bible. The will read every word of it or the Quran and take each word in its literal sense. Worse, still, they will interpret the meaning based on their own ideological filters of ego and what God must have been thinking.*

While these actions may not sound like it is ego centered, the reality is that ego centered people use religion as a means of setting themselves at a higher level than those that do not attend church or attend another "less correct" church.

Again citing concepts by Richard Rohr he discusses people like this as being Gnostic.

Gnostics were "people who knew", and their knowledge

at once constituted them a superior class of beings, whose
present and future status was essentially different from
that of those who, for whatever reason, did not know.
The New Advent Catholic Encyclopedia

Taking and building on this idea to more modern concepts, I have met people that believe that their method of religion, such as Latter day Saints, Catholicism, Lutheranism Judaism, and the like, is the right method to get God to "like" them, and anyone following a different map will not find Heaven and is not loved by the all loving source. This is such a contradiction and yet so many people cannot see this. This thought process almost makes God seem hypocritical, but it is not God. It is the holy humans that only accept those that are on the same religious "team."

They have the inability to see God or Source in life, nature. They do not see God in a dog, or a tree, another human or even themselves. Among the religious orthodox, there were and are those that had a greater awareness.

Grace can only build on nature
Thomas Aquinas

This simple statement from Thomas Aquinas who was a well-known Saint of the Dominican order of the Roman Catholic faith brings nature and grace together. He was born in 1225 and died n 1274. He is widely recognized for his scholarly approach to theological philosophy.

In Christianity, divine grace (Gk. charis)
defined as "unmerited favor" from God. It is the
outpouring of the love of God on humanity
Cross-referenced

Thomas Aquinas clearly ties nature and Gods grace together, yet those that live their lives from the ego-based side of thinking see nature as separate, and are incapable of seeing God in nature. Rohr extrapolates that man has tried to build Grace without connecting it to nature.

> *This is like putting frosting on a non-cake*
> Richard Rohr
> *The Soul, The Natural World, and What is*

People who lead their life egoically have a tendency to see people and religions dualistically, which is to say that they see either good or bad, right or wrong.

They may feel that other religions don't have it right and God must not love "them" as much. They may go so far as to say that a Hindu or Taoist, or Buddhist, or Muslim, or Jew is simply not going to go to Heaven.

There are some that will go to the extreme to even say that a person that is in a different form of Christianity is not as saved as they are. This is the peak of religious arrogance and ego. It occurs in every walk of life, at every socio-economic level and all geographic locations of the globe. A great many wars have begun on this singular thought on God and religion:

> *I am right and you are wrong, and your beliefs must*
> *not be allowed to continue, because they are heresy*

To the ego-centered person, there is only one way to be "saved," and they have it. If others don't do it the same way then they have a moral obligation to either force it upon them or leave them to rot in the pit.

Spirit "real" World

People who live their lives from a spiritual perspective realize that Heaven is here, everyday. It is in the way that they treat each other and the way that they are treated. They don't see Heaven as a place "up there" but that Heaven is found every day in the face of a joyful child or an elderly person. They may find peace on a mountaintop or in the forest connected to nature, or in large crowds of people at a coffee shop.

They also know that hell can be equally as present if they choose. They realize that life is full of circumstances that allow them to see and feel from a perspective that is joyful and loving or angry and fearful.

Absolutely everything that occurs can be seen from this perspective, they see God in everything and everyone.

They see that Joy, Love, Passion, Caring Kindness and the like are God-virtues, and that God is in all creation and that by treating all living organisms as sacred they bring Heaven into existence for all. Imagine if everyone felt this way.

Spiritually driven people see that there is no right or wrong words or rituals to get God to love them.

> *Here is the good news: God loves you despite your*
> *mistakes, despite your "bad" thoughts. YOU ARE*
> *LOVE because you were made in Gods image.*

In fact each of us grow closer to the source and more like it <u>though</u> our mistakes and reflection as we interact and see the true self in all our human flaws as a well as our spiritual perfection.

> *So God created man in his own image, in the image of*
> *God he created him; male and female he created them*
> *Genesis 1:27*

There is nothing in the bible verse about making only certain people in Gods image. It is not the people who worship correctly or only people reading certain bible verses, or singing certain songs, that are made in Gods image. Everyone is made in source image.

People that live in spirit understand that God is love and since we are ALL made in Gods image, then we must ALL be love as well. People that are led this way know that God is love and that they are love. Again quoting Richard Rohr in the CD, An Enneagram Evening,

> *You came forth from God, and you will return to*
> *God, and everything in between in just school*
> *Richard Rohr*
> *An Enneagram Evening*

What a beautiful way to look at life: school. We are here to learn lessons, to teach and serve each other. That's right up my ally.

Those lead by the spirit have learned that you come to God through your mistakes, and your vulnerability, not through perfectly reciting the correct words or genuflecting at the right moment in ceremony. They see God in the darkest moments of their lives, and realize that these are he times that they connect to their spirituality as they surrender to the pain and find God within.

They see that the Bible, and other such verse, while being inspired, was still written by humans and subject to human prejudices, fears, and control... including the decisions made by humans to keep certain books out of it and select those that would serve them appropriately, to go in.

They see that Gods words come from the heart and are born out of love, and humility. It is clear to them that God is not in the words of the Bible but in the silent space between the words. This is the place of contemplation where a person sees deeply inside, that they are a part of a great and loving universe that is all one source; that this source is found in ALL living things if we only see with the eyes of spirit.

While they may not choose to worship in the same manner as others, they find peace in accepting that others are learning their lessons at their own pace. They realize that judging where others are in their lives is not appropriate. Spiritual people do not see others as right and wrong but are accepting of other ideas without necessarily agreeing with them.

Dualistic thinking of right or wrong, good or bad, black and white is not for them to make. These are thoughts of the ego... Not thoughts of the spirit. They accept all as appropriate as long as it is born of the spirit, regardless of the vehicle.

> *It is understood that it is not the type of religion or*
> *worship or even the name of the God, Buddha, Allah,*
> *Ra, that matters, but the depth with which one receives*
> *and gives their spirit that helps them reach fulfillment.*

It is in this way that they may see more of a God image in nature, as there is no right or wrong in nature; there is only acceptance. The idea that God is found in nature is not a new one nor is it pagan.

> *Because that which may be known of God is manifest in*
> *them; for God hath showed it unto them. For the invisible*
> *things of him from the creation of the world are clearly seen,*
> *being understood by the things that are made, even his eternal*
> *power and Godhead; so that they are without excuse*
> Romans 1:19-20

There is no dualism in nature. All is accepted. As Rohr intimates, there are no Presbyterian trees or Catholic mountains. There is only that with which we connect and knowing that, by connecting with nature, we are connecting with Source without any judgment, whole... complete.

Spiritual people know that soul is the realization and recognition of the connection in everything and everyone. The soul may be sought by looking inside, through which we connect to others.

> *Soul is the place that most centrally and comprehensively*
> *identifies a thing- a things truest place... A things*
> *ultimate place corresponds to the set of relationships*
> *that this thing has with all other things in the world.*
> Bill Plotkins
> *Nature and the Human Soul: Cultivating Wholeness*
> *and Community in a Fragmented world*

That is almost identical to the Buddhist definition of Dharma.... That is that Dharma is the ultimate service to others. Those lead by spirit see that our ultimate purpose is the recognition of God in each other and the service that comes from that recognition. They know that any judgments of others are not born of Love and thus are not of God.

The true message of Jesus was of peace and love; not judgment, not fear; not separation.

Turning Point
> *Religion is for people who are afraid of Hell*
> *Spirituality is for people who have already been there*
> *Several credits including*
> *Running Hawk Lakota Nation*
> *Robert G. Ingersoll*
> *Dr. Abraham Twersky*
> *Deepak Chopra*

Realize that God did not make religion. Humans did. God did not write the bible. Many events in the bible were inspired by spiritual incidents, but it was written, translated and edited by humans. Knowing that the decision as to what was to be included in the bible was made by the Nicene council three hundred years after the ascension of Christ means that there were some key components that were removed, or added by humans. The bible is still an invaluable source of God-spirit inspiration, but when we make the words more important than human love, kindness, and joy, we have abused its purpose.

Observe your thoughts and feelings. What is their source? Simply put, if they are not based out of love, peace, joy, it is not of God. If they are motivated by fear, anger, hatred, separation, then they originate from the ego and are not helping you evolve. Realize that this journey is never over and that being humble is a great virtue if you use it as a means to continue to grow and develop.

Catch yourself when you judge others, which may well be human nature. The Buddhists say that what you say about others is really a reflection in some way of how you feel about yourself. Not judging means not judging yourself as well. Be kind to yourself as well as others while trying to learn why certain feelings may arise deep within.

Be kind. There is so much joy found in acts of kindness to others. Perform random acts of kindness to others and you will see just how euphoric you feel. You will feel closer to source and this feeling will self-perpetuate. While you are at it, perform random acts of kindness for yourself, including forgiveness. Forgive yourself for actions and thoughts that may be out of character. Realize your human nature and move on. You will grow and you will continue to learn about yourself.

If you want to find God, realize first that you are a part of the loving source of all, so go inside first. There are a number of ways: prayer, meditation, simply sitting quietly in front of a fireplace or with someone near you in your life. Then realize that everyone and everything is a part of the living source.

If you respond with that mindset the next time someone cuts you off in traffic, you realize that they are just learning their lessons and growing. Don't forget that they are a piece of the all-loving source as well. Returning anger with tolerance is life and love affirming... Therefore, God-affirming.

Reading and learning from truly enlightened people is a powerful source, which leads to greater self-reflection. This includes the bible of course. There are so many sources and I have listed a great many of them in the back of this book.

Finally, realize that your true purpose, your truest connection is always found in the service of others. A movie came out in 2008 called Yes-man, which starred Jim Carey. In this movie the main character was convinced that he had been bound by a covenant to say YES to any opportunity that presented itself in his life. While saying yes to everything did get him in to precarious situations, all of the good in his life occurred when he said yes in service to others.

Realize that there is no perfect religion, for God, Buddha, Allah, Ra did not create any religion. There are no perfect words to say that get you to heaven, for God did not write the Bible, or the Quran. No songs pay the ticket price to the land of milk and honey. All of these things no matter how spiritually inspired they may have been, have also been influenced by humans egos as well.

There is only spirit, and the feelings of joy, love, and acceptance. Dualistic thinking, right and wrong, good or bad, do not exist except in the minds of humans.

> *There's No color lines or casts or classes...Whatever faith you*
> *practice. Whatever you believe... There ain't no walls around*
> *heaven... There are no codes you gotta know to get in...*
> *You cannot buy your salvation... The failure keeps you humble*
> *Leads us closer to peace*
> *Brett Dennen*
> *Song: Heaven*
> *Source: Absolutely Lyrics*

These lyrics above from Brett Dennen's song Heaven, really say it all. How often we look at someone else's social class, and say, "well, they'll never get to Heaven," as if Heaven were a place, or we feel like we can buy our way in.

The only payment required is failure, which leads us closer to our truest self. There are no church services that are the one and only way. Whenever religion gets in the way of your relationship with God, you have gone to ego.

It is not the words, or money, or classes, or buildings, but rather the inspiration of love behind these things that are the true meaning of religion. Celebrate the awareness of who we truly are... connected by the greatest power in the Universe... Love.

The next time you have the urge to judge someone because they go to another church or their church is a mountain or forest look inside. If you are not motivated from spirit, if your thoughts are not of love, then they probably will only hurt. They are driven of ego. Remember that pride is one of the 7 deadly sins.

Instead of being offended, be grateful that people have found a connection to spirit. Be joyful in the knowledge that we are all connected through spirit regardless of the method that we use to see it.

Entitlement

Bow to the Princess
Bumper sticker

PRESUMABLY, THIS WAS IN jest but even so, there is intention in this statement that we see more and more these days. I coach and teach pre-college teens and I have become aware of a rising belief of entitlement among youth, and adults.

We have become a society of people that feel that we "deserve" to have certain things. In sports, it is the top of the batting order or the starting pitcher, or quarterback, or point guard. And at certain levels of play, we "deserve" the division one college scholarship.

In school, I have students that come to me to explain that they "deserve" an A because they tried hard. Often their parents advocate for them and become irate if I do not acquiesce. While at the same time teachers are under microscopes of standardized test scores, due to the prevailing political whims of the way the No child left behind laws are enforced.

At work we "deserve" a raise, because we have been at a certain place of employment for a long period of time. Not because we have earned it or have taken on extra responsibilities. We become upset when our evaluator does not see things that way.

At the national level, as Americans, we "deserve" respect from other countries, and the right to consume resources, pollute land, air and sea, force our will upon other countries because we can. We stand behind the American flag as if it awarded us immunity from being decent humans and treating everyone with respect. We use the word patriotism as a tool to command respect. Not earn respect... command it... because we deserve it. As a race we have forgotten that the way to gain respect is by respecting others first. The sense of entitlement has engulfed our existence.

People have confused the idea of deserve with the idea of desire. They have lost the understanding that into every award has gone a great deal of effort. People have lost sight of gaining respect by first respecting others without judging them.

> *Today, the biggest challenge we must meet is the one we*
> *present to ourselves. To not become a nation that places*
> *entitlement ahead of accomplishment. To not become*
> *a country that places comfortable lies ahead of difficult*
> *truths. To not become a people that thinks so little of*
> *ourselves that we demand no sacrifice from each other.*
> Chris Christie
> New Jersey Governor

Ego "real" World

The ego based person looks at the physical world as if they are owed something at all times. They feel strongly that they "deserve" the best salary, the best house, the largest car, and so on. They see others success and feel that this type of thing is owed to them as well.

They do not see the effort, training, and energy that went into the other person's level of accomplishment. They only see success in terms of power and monetary prowess. They feel that in order to succeed, others must fall rather than raising everyone up. There is no value in helping others that they may be in "competition" with. Theirs is a perspective of limitations; that there are only so many pieces of the pie and in order to get theirs, someone else must lose. There is no understanding of abundance.

Ego-centered humans have been taught their entire lives that they are owed things and that it is acceptable to simply take what is "theirs" regardless of if this hurts another.

This results in the manner with which we approach the homeless, third world countries, and global disasters. We take on the idea of "at least it was someone else." Instead of reaching out to those in need, they are only looking for what they deserve and turning a blind eye to others.

I was on a social network about six months after the Haitian earthquake in 2010. There was a charitable relief organization advertising for assistance and one of the people in my friendship community stated that she was tired of hearing about Haiti and wished that people would stop giving to them. It was her contention that people should only give their money to the needs of the United States. While, on the surface this appears to be somewhat forthright. This is the "me" first approach, even in a manner that seems to be altruistic, but only to "our group." This is still a position of ego: "We deserve" mentality is the same, as "I deserve."

Those living in the ego-world move about, taking from others with no thought of gratitude or contriteness. They have been taught to believe that others are only here to serve them.

Spirit "real" World

> *Saying thank you is more than good*
> *manners. It is good spirituality.*
> *Alfred Painter*

Those that live their lives from the spiritual perspective understand that all things that come their way are necessary for them, at that moment in time. They are grateful for this and they know that everything occurs as a piece of the cosmic puzzle that is placed in our lives as a means to grow, learn or raise others up. While their external lives may not reflect the standards of worldly "success" that others do, they are content with simply being of service and find richness in that.

People living from this perspective get that one of the most important aspects of our lives is the ability to serve others. The Hindu call this Karma.

This is a concept that we must be cautious of. If the only reason that we serve others is so that we get paid back in the future, like some sort of good cosmic bank deposit, then we are actually approaching this from the perspective of ego. The reason that spirit driven people serve others is because they understand that this is what is best for the universe, and they receive a particular joy from this. This joy is derived from serving our spiritual brothers and sisters.

The physical world is a place for them to add benefit to by their presence, thoughts, feelings, and actions. They approach life with joy and absolutely care about others success. Their interaction with others leaves everyone feeling better about life, and humanity, because their singular purpose is about giving, not taking.

People of spirit are not afraid to go to work and see the value in the journey not so much the destination. Grades, pay raises, accolades and the like come to them because they are willing to put in the effort and the energy to earn them, and because they receive joy in the person that they become along the way. They are grateful for everything that comes into their lives.

These are the people that will stop to help push a stalled car off the road in the middle of an intersection, or lend a hand to friend when they are moving furniture. They never look for rewards for these actions… only the opportunity to serve.

By the way these people also make the best leaders in society. Many of these are teachers, religious leaders, and the like. They are not limited, however, to altruistic professions. They may be small business owners of successful companies, even CEOs.

Most recently founder and former CEO of Apple, Steve Jobs passed away. At the Apple store in Chicago, and I would presume all over the United States, there were thousands of sticky notes placed on the window of the Company front with sentiments regarding Steve and that he will be missed. My understanding is that he was demanding but fair, and was successful, not just because of the innovations that he brought, but because he helped others become successful. The most successful businesses, communities, athletic teams, and so on, always have a common denominator. They had leaders that realized that the key to leadership was not by pushing or pulling but by lifting others to the higher level. They are revered within the ranks for generations that follow. Never did they act as if their employees or teammates owed them anything. Never did they act as if they were entitled!

By definition, a push or a pull is force, while we use power to raise others. Once again, reinforcing the idea that power is greater than force.

Turning Point

Moving to the spirit-based perspective is not easy because we are lead to believe through commercials that we "deserve" the good things in life, that we are more special than others. We see this in events as simple as when we are driving and another person cuts us off on the road or when someone parks their vehicle in such a way so as to take up more than one space in a crowded parking lot. We are often offended at this because we feel that we "deserve" better treatment.

So how do we turn this toward spirit? If you view each person as an extension of God, as if they were your brother and sister, that goes a long way to changing the perspective of separation. Remember that we were made in Gods image... Not some of us... All of us! I am not sure about others, but I find a great deal of motivation to serve Source, rather than demand from Source. I am grateful for the opportunity.

In this way we are extensions of each other. We are all from the same source. We are all the same. Therefore, by helping others we are raising the energy flow and fulfilling your Dharma. How you treat others is how you treat yourself. That may be beneficial or not but it is a reflection of how you feel about yourself!

Look no farther than even the New Testament of the Bible. In all of the writings about Jesus, we see him serving others. He refused service from others. He was deeply humble and contrite. His life exemplified service, joy, peace, and forgiveness... love. At no time did he seem offended by others.

> *But I tell you. Do not resist an evil person. If someone strikes you on the right cheek, turn to him the other also*
> Matthew 5:39

It would seem that this is a great example of a way to view entitlement. If anyone should have had a sense of entitlement, it would have been the Son of God. Often Jesus referred to himself as the Son of man and looked at others as his brothers and sisters. He realized that the best form of leadership was in raising others up; not for what he got out of the "deal" but because he knew that this would evolve all of human kind.

As a result of his selflessness, he has been revered by a great many cultures for thousands of years. He gave the ultimate sacrifice instead of saving himself and being hailed by all around him, because he was "entitled" to.

It boils down to one simple action: service. Service to others whereby we raise others for no other reason other than to move all of humanity forward into love, peace, joy and abundance. There is no shortage. There is abundance only. By serving we bring abundance to all.

Victims Or Learners

*This is what I know for certain: We may rest in
the assurance that no experience comes to punish
or test us; experiences come to awaken us
Michael Bernard Beckwith
The Answer is You*

EVERY DAY OF OUR physical existence affords us with opportunities to interact with new circumstances. Often these are viewed in a negative manner. These may be what many would call small annoyances like breaking a shoelace, or scrapping our knee, to what people would call large catastrophes, like losing a job, or a loved one passing over to the spiritual realm, being a victim of a crime. Some would call these "bad" or "horrible." They are neither. These terms imply judgment. Who are we to judge the universe? Let us use the term, challenges.

In the physical world, we are presented with challenges on a daily basis. Sometimes challenges come in adversarial form through interaction of physical beings, particularly in large cities. Some people choose to isolate themselves or their children from these. Some people turn away from them, some try to fight them still others welcome them.

Challenges can sometimes crop up on us and seem to come one after another. Often times, they are the same challenge in a different form. As people experience life they may be faced with physical challenges such as arthritis, or muscle weakness, brain traumas, and other physiological ailments. Over the course of life, challenges may be more emotional such as losing jobs, loved ones, divorce.

Everyone has different challenges and all affect people in various ways. Some are more important than others and some seem trivial. It is the way that we see each challenge and how we use them to develop our ultimate existence on this journey that really matters.

The way that a person responds to, what they view as a challenge is very telling as to their perspective. Some may see themselves as victims, and are always expecting the worse to happen to them next. They are often gloomy and tend to expect bad "luck."

On the other hand there are those that will look at life's "challenges" as simply an opportunity to grow and learn more about their true self. They believe that everything happens for a purpose. Their perspective teaches them that each experience brings them closer to their true self and that of others.

Ego "real" World

> *This accumulated pain is a negative energy field that*
> *occupies your body and mind. If you look on it as*
> *an invisible entity in its own right, you are getting*
> *quite close to the truth. It's the emotional pain body.*
> *It has two modes of being: dormant and active.*
> *The pain body wants to survive, just like every other*
> *entity in existence, and it can only survive if it gets you to*
> *unconsciously identify with it. It can then rise up, take you*
> *over, "become you," and live through you. It needs to get*
> *its "food" through you. It will feed on any experience that*
> *resonates with its own kind of energy, anything that creates*
> *further pain in whatever form: anger, destructiveness,*
> *hatred, grief, emotional drama, violence, and even illness*
> *Eckhart Tolle'*
> *A New Earth*
> *Awakening to Your Life's Purpose*

The previous passage by Eckhart Tolle' is his description of the <u>Pain-Body.</u> It is a part of the ego and is fed and lives by pain. Those in ego existence identify with the Pain-Body.

Those that participate in life from the ego perspective view challenges from the basis of fear. They see these interactions from the victim perspective. They will adopt the "why me?" perspective. Yet they unconsciously see the Pain-Body as a part of who they are. If they are perpetually ill, then this is their ego identity and may actually need this as part of who they think they are. If they see them selves as accident prone, then this becomes a part of their ego identity. Their pain body identifies them, even though they will publicly deny it. They feel that there is no escaping it, and they are right, in the sense that they want to hide from it, and cannot ever do so.

They take everything personally and view challenges as something to either acquiesce to or overcome, even if neither ever actually occurs. They see only a fight or flight response of the adrenal gland, which evolved as a means to protect our bodies during times of physical threat. They must combat or run from their challenges.

> *They could never surrender into or think that*
> *spirit is found in these challenges.*

Everything in their life is seen dualistically as good-bad, enemy-friend. From the person in traffic that they are competing with, to the caring individual in a grocery store that offered to let them move ahead in line, ego-centered individuals only see life's challenges or participants as being "on" their side or not. This is the so-called friend or foe that constantly keeps us separate and allows the ego to thrive!

Spirit "real" World

The person that lives from a spirit perspective sees challenges in life as an opportunity to learn and grow. Each new event is only a lesson to be learned and to grow closer to their true being. When stuff "happens" the spiritually focused person realizes that they are soulful students here for only a short stretch of geological time to enhance this life, to love, and to have the physical experience and find Dharma.

Even the most challenging moments are seen to be a new lesson, and they increase their awareness to see the good. Even the death of a loved one, the onset of powerful diseases and more are viewed with an open mind and an open heart.

They realize that there is a perfect symphonic harmony to large and small incidents. They realize that the perfection of a situation may not be realized immediately or ever but they know that the interaction is as it should be, or it would not have ever occurred.

They stand vigilant to realize what each challenge has to teach them and they know that challenges will always bring out the best in them and help them to rise to a new level of awareness. Where others see attackers, the spiritually based person sees teachers.

The loving woman in my life found a quote that most represents what spiritual people understand about life's challenges. I cannot express this any better.

> *You will not grow if you sit in a beautiful flower garden,*
> *But you will grow if you are sick, if you are in pain, if you*
> *Experience losses, and if you do not put your head in the sand,*
> *But take the pain and learn to accept it, not as a curse or*
> *Punishment but as a gift to you with*
> *a very very specific purpose.*
> *Elisabeth Kubler-Ross*
> *Growth Through Pain*

Turning Point

Like everyone, I have had my share of challenges in life. It is not easy but I have tried always to see how I may grow from these situations. No one grows and becomes more internally aware of their own one-ness when everything in life is smooth, and they have no emotional, or physical challenges, or they have all of the money that they could ever wish for.

In the same way that sports teams do not truly attempt to correct mistakes when they win games, people in general need to have what they perceive as challenges in order to develop a greater awareness and spirituality. Some challenges can seem minor, and others, life-altering.

> *A bad day for the ego is a good day for the soul*
> *Michael Bernard Beckwith*
> *Spiritual Liberation*

Challenges are in our lives for a reason. We don't always see, clearly, what that reason is at the time that events are taking place, but when I look back at the times of greatest change in my life, it has *always* been during the difficult challenges of my life. I am still learning to let go and surrender to these moments and look for the opportunities that are offered from within.

It is not easy, because our ego wants to hold onto the Pain-Body. God is offering an opportunity for me to rid my life of the past dead weight and lighten my heart toward the realization of my true self. It is important, in these times to ask the spirit the following questions/ statements and meditate on the answer:

1. *What is the lesson?*
2. *How may I grow?*
3. *Show me the way to be grateful.*

Be sure to listen for the response, because it will appear but spiritual answers are almost always subtle.

The tendency, when we feel the challenges in our lives, is to focus on the pain that they may cause, but pain is there to get your attention, so that you focus on what needs to improve.

Go to the pain. Step inside of it and
listen to the spiritual whisper

Seek the lesson and apply the necessary improvements. Most importantly, be grateful, not only for this gift but for all of the gifts in your life. There are many gifts: your ability to think, to breathe, to love, and many others.

Focus on the beauty, and what you thought
was "bad" will turn out to be a gift.

Look at the people who are your teachers. Who are the best teachers? I classify three types of life teachers.

1. Those that appear to be responsible for your challenges, and put you in a position to learn the lesson.
2. Those that teach by counseling us in difficulty and point us in positive directions.
3. Those that teach us by being that which is spiritual.

<u>Teachers who appear to put the challenges before us.</u> These are people that many would call our "enemies" or antagonists. Through some action of theirs we feel offended or attacked. Examples may be the aggressive driver drives fast and gets very close to your rear bumper in traffic, or someone who stares at you in a bar or gym. There is nothing like a little alcohol or testosterone to magnify an ego-centered situation. Sometimes they are friends or family members that disagree with a point of view.

There are a great many examples like this. Anything that makes a person want to push back because of the perceived "offense" of the situation is an opportunity to learn from someone. How do you respond to people like this? Do you attack, or "do what is right" when someone appears in this situation? Do you ever reach out to them? This is amazingly powerful.

Do you feel the need to win an argument? Think about these words by Dr. Dyer the next time that you are in an argument in which each party has a differing perspective:

> *Do I want to be right or do I want to be happy?*
> *Wayne Dyer*
> *Power of Intention*

What do we really gain by proving ourselves right and another wrong? Do you feel good down through your toes or have you simply satisfied the egos needs?

Many people who feel the need to be "right" have a good intention. An example may be an evangelist that wants to save someone by showing him or her the "right" way to love God. Their intention is to help someone because they believe that the methods they use to worship God is a better way or the only way to be saved. Can you see the dualistic thinking in this?

To grow from this kind of teaching, a person must recognize it for what it is. The key is to get passed our egos and look at how this helps us to grow in a spiritual manner. The use of self-reflection, meditation, looking for the feeling place will help us to move toward illumination.

I am grateful to my most challenging teachers in life. I have learned that reaching out to them is one of the most healing things that a person can do.

I may have felt like a victim at the time but as I reflect back on those moments in my life, they were the moments of he greatest transformation in my spirit and recognition of who I really am. They are often very painful at the time but through that pain, I have seen more light in myself and in others than any time in my life.

Again, I reflect on the words that have helped me to understand this pain, that were passed on to me so many years ago:

> *When you feel pain, that's just God clearing away*
> *the dead unnecessary branches of our lives*
> *Fr. James Koenigsfeld*

<u>Teachers who teach through advice:</u> I remember my parents attempting to do so. When I was a teen, I did not listen very well. The older I grew, the more that I realized the sage wisdom that left their mouths as easily as water off a fall, as well as the love that motivated their pearls of care.

Others may include friends, family members, and yes, counselors. The best of these types of teachers are those that have actually experienced the same type or similar type of challenge that you are going through. It is very difficult to heed a person's advice if they cannot relate to your experience. Those that have surrendered to the pain, gone inside and come out on the other side having learned from and grown from their pain are valuable teachers.

<u>Teachers that teach us by the way that they live their lives:</u> I feel like I can best illustrate this by telling the story of Dave. This is an ongoing story as Dave is so vibrant with life today that you can actually see the light in and around him.

I met Dave at the gym where I work out every morning at five am about three years ago. We started participating in spin class together on Fridays and after seeing him on a daily basis we introduced ourselves.

Dave is in his late fifties. He lives life to the fullest by the way that he obviously cares about people and the joyful demeanor with which he carries himself. I see him working out bright and early every day. He is retired from the police department. When he is not working out he spends time traveling with his wife or going to the local college games.

Every day I walk into the gym, I make a beeline to Dave who is always on an elliptical rider at that time. I love chatting to him. He is kind and cares, and genuinely listens to people with interest. To say the least, Dave has mastered the art of being present. More than that, it is uplifting to be in his presence. He clearly has the light of God and shares it with all around him.

This would be enough to simply hold Dave up as a model of teaching how to live life. But more that that, Dave was diagnosed in 1987 with a degenerative brain disease. You can barely detect it when he speaks in the slight drawl of some of his words, or when he has some balance issues. Many people would look at this as a situation to feel like a victim, but apparently, Dave sees this as an opportunity to focus on joy, and light and an opportunity to spread that to the others around him. I truly look up to him, and see him as a direct extension of the way I would see God. What a great teacher.

Another example of being a great teacher by being an example is my brother Dan. At the age of eleven, Dan was stricken with polio. This was a prevalent disease in children during the nineteen forties and fifties. Daniel lost the use of his legs because of this. Since he was the oldest in the family and I was the youngest there was eighteen years between us. I grew up looking up to him. He *never* used the lack of functional legs as an excuse not to accomplish something.

My sister tells me a story about how he and she were surprised on the streets of Chicago by would-be muggers. The muggers must have been shocked when this supposed easy mark of a "cripple" and a young girl turned on them. According to my sister, he knocked both of the muggers out with his crutches.

Daniel was the leader in the church choir playing his folk version of music that inspired so many people and which was modeled after the likes of the Kingston Trio and Simon and Garfunkel. He was a banker but decided to make it on his own as a financial planner and was highly successful. He married an amazing woman, and raised two incredible kids.

In our family he was our second dad. We all looked to him for guidance and strength. I could go on and on about how he was an inspiration of the life that was clearly inspired by God. He was amazing. In March of 2000 he passed of cancer. It was devastating to our family but even in his passing we saw the inspiration in all of the people whose lives he affected. While in the midst of cancer treatments during an ever-slipping prognosis, he spent extra energy to crack jokes and put the rest of the family at ease... that was his nature.

A third example of this type of teacher is, generally speaking, elderly people. As I have developed arthritic hips and back due to overuse, I have learned to slow down. I do believe that examples of this are simply a means of the source to express to us the importance of slowing down and truly being present, since we rarely find the means to do so ourselves, among all of the activity of the "real" world.

The gift of pain points out a very important lesson. I look at these physical pains as a means to bring my focus to the present and hence see them as gifts. As I become more aware of my present, I notice people more. I look in their eyes and I smile. You can tell a great deal about someone's ability to be present by the look in his or her eye.

> *Beautiful young people are accidents of nature,*
> *but beautiful old people are works of art*
> Eleanor Roosevelt

More often than not, when I look at the face and into the eyes of an elderly person, I see the light of the universe. There is joy, and awareness, and more importantly, there is recognition of each other as coming from a similar place. There is recognition, at the spiritual level, of our common source... It is almost as if my spirit and theirs wave at each other in the common realization that we are simply undergoing this temporary physical experience. We are all from the same neighborhood.

To take this even deeper, I hold up my father as a shining example of this understanding. He may have been the greatest teacher I have ever had. As his body grew older, he clearly became more joyful. As his nighttime caregiver, I was acutely aware that his body was in constant pain, and yet he grew more joyful, happier, more spiritual, and more present.

His presence grew to be greater than simple spiritual recognition in those around him. He became present on another level. When he smiled, it was as warm and universal as if God were smiling directly at you. Total strangers could see the light in him. He was beloved by everyone.

As the life was leaving his body at the age of ninety-two, in June of 2011, all of his children took time away from their lives to be at his bedside. Hospice had set up a bed in his living room at the home were I spent a great deal of my life.

He was not sad; he was not in emotional pain. His consciousness fluttered back and forth from physical to spiritual. As I witnessed it, I was and still am certain that he was visiting mom and Daniel on a spiritual level. You could not be in his presence at this time and not feel the spiritual energy.

When a brand new hospice nurse showed up to check on him and explain things to him she introduced herself to dad, and the very first thing that he did was open his arms to hug her. He was hardly coherent enough to speak but he hugged her in recognition.

While his physical body still maintained the life force, I am certain that he was pure love at that moment. I am glad that he chose not to go to a hospice care location... That he wanted to stay with us until he "gave up the ghost" as was his euphemism.

I feel so blessed that I had that time with him, although it was extremely emotional to have his physical presence cross over to spiritual. Even as I write these words, I have begun to weep at the loss of his physical presence.

The time that I spent with him during the last years of his life is as precious a time as I can think of. For six and a half years I was his evening caregiver. We reconnected on a level that was incredibly deep. When we laughed, it was a deep thundering laugh, and when we cried it was heartfelt and pure. I miss that physical interaction but am blessed for the time that we had.

If anyone is looking for a way to see the truest level of spirituality, to have a teacher that can show them the way to "see the face of God," I encourage them to spend time with the elderly; particularly their own elderly family members. It is surprising how much we seem to take for granted the presence of people in our lives, their experience, and their wisdom until they have departed this physical plane. You will see the light of God in their faces.

Are there still some that have held the fears and ego-centered perspective over the years? Certainly, but it has been my experience that most have found a way to surrender to spirit. Maybe the people, who have not, just need someone to care enough to partake in their lives.

It was the one of the greatest blessings of my life to share the time I did with my dad and I realize how much it has changed my world. In life and in passing, his dedication to his wife has left me with a shining model in which to fashion my own spirit. The love that they shared was born of God and nothing short.

From which perspective do you view life's little and big challenges? Everything that happens and I mean everything can be a lesson in the making, even if you don't see the lesson at the time.

The most important thing that you do may be to be present in the moment and surrender to it. Don't judge it, and don't analyze it... just be with it. All events have helped to shape the way that you view the "real" world. *Know* that you always have the choice to see things from any perspective.

I am not trying to convince you that when large events occur, such as deaths, or being fired from a job, do not warrant emotional responses. We are all human.... Give yourself a break and experience all of those emotions fully and totally. You can even feel sorry for yourself. But then, stop, search, surrender then look, and see the lesson, or find the part of you that is awakened by the event and how you can grow spiritually from it.

> *Trust that this is another opportunity to increase*
> *your awareness and bring you into the light.*

Find excitement in where this new set of circumstances will take your life. Find teachers and thank them. Grow, and never stop. It is not punishment... It is opportunity to become enlightened and to move forward in spiritual evolution. It is one more step toward your ultimate purpose.

God Image

The feeling remains that God is on the journey, too
Teresa of Avila
Roman Catholic Saint, Spanish mystic, Writer

WHAT DO YOU THINK of when I say God? Morgan Freeman? George Burns? As children, we are often presented with an image of a stately old man garnished with a beard and white robe and gold sash, sitting on a throne in a cloud with a scorecard in hand. On the scorecard are places to make checks. If you do something "good" you get a "good" check mark, but if you do something "bad" then you get a "bad" check mark. At the end of your life, if you have more "good" than "bad" check marks, you get to pass the Pearly gates and enter the kingdom of Heaven. If not, then you don't. The dualism leaps out immediately.

As humans with limited awareness of our consciousness we are constantly attempting to classify, and categorize. We seem to have the need to put things in boxes and in neat little packages. For a child that is not taught to look within, that is not taught to think from the heart, it is these simplistic images that adults often use to "explain" God. These images, all too often are used to teach children to behave appropriately... "Better behave or God will punish you."

What an uninspired means of explaining the common source of our being. These images stick with us, unless we seek more awareness.

Unfortunately, we only tend to seek when we are stretched beyond our comfort zone.

So how do you see God? Is God a being? Is God energy, a thought? Is God punishing and spiteful? Should we fear God? Should we love God? These are questions that can only be answered from within.

If you believe that God is a punishing, spiteful being that is constantly looking at your mistakes, then you will go through life living in fear and guilt. If you believe that God is benevolent, loving, peaceful, joyful, then you will react to this by caring and loving others in a joyful manner. You will see God in everyone and everything.

Being raised and taught through the Catholic perspective, I, more often than not, conjured fear and guilt when God was brought to mind. I felt an *obligation* to be a "good" person, because if I did not, then God would give me a "bad" checkmark, or worse, strike me down right where I stood.

Attending confession was an all-together, guilt-inducing experience. While in conference with a priest, we were to recall all of the "bad" things that we had done, and the priest would assign us a number of prayers as penance for our sins. After that, all would be fine.

My recollection of this upbringing was never focused on how beautiful and loving God was. Rarely did the clergy ever speak about God as the loving, beautiful, caring, forgiving Source of all being. We were taught to fear the wrath of God. I never understood, why I should fear the very entity that brought all the gifts to my life. Didn't "he" want me to love him?

I recognize, now that the word fear in scripture was a poor translation of the real meaning. That this was more of an attempt to teach respect born from love. Over thousands of years there have been many translations into every language. This has skewed some of the meaning because many languages do not offer direct word translations from Hebrew and Latin. Additionally, there were decisions to keep some writings out of the bible while keeping others.

There is a vast history of all churches and religions. Most of them at one time or another in their history, imposed their ideas (often violently) about God on other people. I have never felt that God wanted anyone killed in "his" name, yet this has taken place millions of times over the millennia of human existence.

So how is God manifested in our lives?

Ego "real" World

From an ego perspective, God is watching constantly, and judging your every move, thought, feeling. He punishes you if you are "bad" and rewards you if you are "good."

When life is troubling and difficult then God is punishing you in the way that he punished Job, but when life is good, you have plenty of money or the love of your life appears, then God must be rewarding you.

So often people view God in this psychological behavioral modification model because this is how we were raised. This is carried through to the adult psyche and people who seem to get whatever they want and have the "perfect" life are seen as being favored by the almighty. A homeless person, however, would be modern days version of Job being punished for his sins... although that was not the lesson of the book of Job , it is how so many people see God today.

Those driven by ego, take biblical "fear of God" to a literal level. To them there is only one way to see God and it is blasphemy to think of God in any other way than the way he is depicted in the Old Testament. There are biblical fundamentalists that take every word as literal.

Their "respect" for God is strictly that of extrinsic control by a being that sees all and knows all. Because of this they "behave" appropriately in accordance with scripture. This is the child-rearing model and they feel that by doing the "right" things they will earn their ticket to Heaven.

> *When a person abandons the impositions of external*
> *authority, and becomes their own, self-directed*
> *authority, then they become far more functional in the*
> *world. This is , in fact a higher state of consciousness,*
> *one which provides a higher vista of awareness.*
> Owen Waters
> The Shift

They do not see the intrinsic drive to love one another. They are not grateful for every day as being a gift. This translates into the ultimate "right" and "wrong."

They have no issue with war or death in any way as long as "we" are right and the other guy is "wrong." The death penalty is the ultimate in Gods punishment for misbehavior... an eye for an eye.

God is "out there" and it is up to use to do his will, so we can go to the "good" place.

Spirit "real" World

> *We were born to make manifest the glory of God that is*
> *within us. It's not just in some of us; it's in all of us. And*
> *when we let our own light shine, we unconsciously give other*
> *people permission to do the same. As we are liberated from*
> *our own fear, our presence automatically liberates others*
> Marianne Williamson
> A Return to Love: reflections on the
> Principles of a Course in Miracles
> Used by Nelson Mandela in his 1994 inaugural speech

The spiritually centered person sees God in everything and everywhere. They see that heaven is not a place but more a state of flow in the heart and consciousness and can experience it every day if they choose it.

> *They feel God by responding with love to all*
> *situations in life and understand that by doing*
> *so they bring God into all situations.*

This helps them to evolve when challenges arrive in their life rather than seeing it as Gods wrath. They may feel that God is everything, that God is all matter, and energy, and the greatest form of energy is Love. They understand that God has purpose and it is their desire to accept the purpose and allow the lesson, which is not always clear. That is called faith. While the lesson or purpose of circumstances may not be clear, a spiritually minded person accepts the situation and finds growth to awareness in everything.

> *Advanced theoretical physics demonstrated that everything*
> *in the universe is subtly dependent on everything else*
> *David Hawkins*
> *Power VS. Force*
> *Citing Power in the Arts*

Their control is intrinsic. They feel the love energy that is God and because of this are motivated to treat all of their brothers and sisters with respect and care. They know that this has a positive effect on the entire universe.

> *They may view everything as God, and come to the realization*
> *that God is the loving power that connects all of us in spirit*

They know that God is within as well as all that surrounds them, and feel that whenever they are inspired to create. Those motivated by spirit ask, constantly, what is my highest purpose, and seek, with compassion and passion, to fulfill this.

They know that there is no force outside of themselves waiting to punish them for being "bad" and reward them for being "good."

Theirs is to seek awakening and no longer wish to await this blessing but to look to the spirit for loving guidance to the highest power. Many would call this Heaven.

To the spirit-driven, God is not a thunder from
on high, but rather a whisper from within

The person that is filled with spirit may see God as the energy in which we are made from, and are completely immersed in. In the same way that a fish is not aware of the water in which it swims, we are not aware of the God that is everything and speaks to us from the spirit within, and that in which we participate every moment of existence

The spiritually centered also see that God-spirit is calm, kind, joyful, giving and creative.

They may find God in the inspiration that they are given to paint, or learn an instrument, or write. Their perspective teaches them that anything that is <u>creative and serving</u> comes from the loving connection that is God.

<u>Turning Point</u>

He who does not love, does not know God, for God is love
1 john 4:8

What an inspired statement! What a beautiful image to have of our source... Love! Bring love to all situations in life. Be lovingly present, and you are with God.

By this all will know that you are my disciples,
if you have love for one another
John 13:35

There are so many ways to celebrate God by living in the spirit. When you feel inspired to do something that is joyful, listen to it.

The way of God is subtle and as you receive the
whispers of inspiration they are leading you to a higher
level of awareness.... All we need do is listen.

Learn to see God in everyone and everything. Start small and see God in the face of a child, or a puppy. Look at the face, and more importantly into the eyes of the elderly. Most of them have been away from the "rat race" of the slow-energy, physical world long enough and have returned their focus to the natural, real world of spirit. It is apparent when you look deep inside their eyes. Try to extend this to the person in the car next to you. If you approach everyone with the love of Source, the same Source that brought everything into being, it changes the way that you treat people.

Here is an example: You hurry to the bank to make a deposit but are running behind schedule. You park and begin to head inside but as you approach the door, someone pulls up in their car and parks illegally by the door, and gets in line before you do. They then proceed to occupy the teller for ten minutes. As you wait for your turn you begin to think how you could already be done with your transaction by now and be on your way if this person had not "broken the rules." Many of us might react verbally or silently with some sort of expletive regarding the person that "cut" in front of us, and their personality or intelligence level.

Instead of reacting this way, try to picture the person as an extension of your very Source. How would you respond if that were actually God? Sort of changes the perspective. Wouldn't you forgive them? I have found this to be a life-changing act... Although, like everyone, I still have a lot of work to do.

Here is the really neat part: Many times when I might have responded to someone in an ego-centered manner in which the other person "offended" me, I caught myself. I would change my perspective of that person and see them as God, The loving creator of life! The other person usually senses the change in energy and they feel welcomed. We might end up introducing ourselves, or even learning more about each other than we ever thought we would before this change. We recognize the true selves in each other and greet as if there were a bond between us.

By realizing that God, Allah, Ra, Source is not out to punish you, is not a puppeteer, and only wants you to learn the lesson of love by <u>sharing with and serving each other</u>, and by treating ALL life as sacred, and being present in each moment, you learn to love God and savor the moment. By doing so, you are in Heaven, and God is always by your side.

> *But, as it is written, "What no eye has seen, nor*
> *ear heard, nor the heart of man imagined, what*
> *God has prepared for those who love him"*
> 1 Corinthians 2:9

Section 4:
What, How, Why

In the previous section, I discussed some common situations that can be viewed from spirit or ego based perspectives. Why in the world am I writing this book? How do we go about meshing spirit into a world that is highly ego based? Why in the world should it happen? What is the "real" world?

What Is The Real World?

Show me the face you had before your parents were born
Buddhist Koan

So now, I return to one of my early stories, about my friend asking me how I know what is going on in the "real" world. I ask you all, what is the "real" world? Is it the ego-based, I only believe what I see, there is only a certain amount of the pie, and I must get mine, how dare they do that to me, if you don't worship the same way as I then you are wrong, we get our way or we kick your butt, consuming more and wasting more makes me happy, who cares about the environment or anyone else, dualistic, right and wrong, physical world?

Or is your world that of a more spiritual foundation, that sees each being as experiencing their own lessons, seeking their own Dharma and living that the best way that they can, finding ways to help each other and raise them up, allowing others to find spirituality within and *know* the connection that we all have to each other and to source, finding ways to see peace and love as far more powerful than fear and anger, understanding that we are all spiritual beings undergoing this temporary physical experience?

The spiritual world is not a thinking place. It is a feeling place. It is a place of Love, joy, caring, presence. We all enter these feelings from time to time. Some enter them more than others. When we feel love deep inside, when we become overwhelmed with a sense of joy, when caring for someone or several others becomes a feeling of euphoria, we have entered the purest feeling of spirit. Very often these spiritual feelings can leave us in tears of inexplicable joy. Once we have experienced this we seek it again. All too often we look outside ourselves for it, when it is actually found within.

Which of those is actually more "real?" What is "real?" Is it only what you can perceive with your five senses, or is it deeper than that? In the physical world, we cannot see, feel, smell, taste, or hear, unaided, a large portion of the electromagnetic spectrum, yet we have a belief that radio waves, and many other forms of energy exist. We cannot see gravity, yet we feel it to be real. Why should the spiritual world be any less real? Is it because we can measure gravitational pull using force meters, but you have no way of numerically quantifying the feeling place?

David Hawkins would disagree with that in <u>Power VS. Force.</u> His book is all about the quantifiable measurement, and he has spent decades supporting his scientific findings in the most rigorous and systematic ways possible, in science. As a scientist myself, I am very impressed with the extent that Hawkins went to in order to verify his findings.

If the real world is deeper, then where do we find it? Which is a world that you want to be part of? Is the "real" world the one that we choose? Does it choose us, and we simply have no say? Is it something in between ego and spirit? How do we strive for one or the other?

I know which one I would choose, but is it realistic to think that anyone can live completely in one or the other? I think that there are some that have nearly mastered the ego world, and that there are some Zen masters, and other spiritual students that have nearly mastered the spirit-based world. Is it possible to "think" in one world and "feel" in the other? These questions, while rhetorical, are also contemplative in nature, and are decisions that we must all make. If you have not already contemplated this, perhaps this is a good time to do so.

> *I truly believe that where you live and how you see*
> *the world is completely a choice that we make and*
> *results from our ability to "tune in" to self-awareness,*
> *and our desire to live a life of service to all life*

Is it easy to live in the ego world? It does not appear so. It seems that everything is comprised of conflict, anger, fear, winners, losers, right, and wrong, destruction, and the like... Whew! That seems like a stressful way of living. Some people seem to do well with that but not me. I really don't believe that my heart could take that perspective all the time... how about yours?

Is it easier to live in the spirit world? It may, perhaps, be more joyful, but there is, initially a re-thinking process to take place. There is a cognitive, and spiritual "rewiring" to help us direct our thoughts to the feeling place in the heart, rather than in the logical, structural, ego place, which we all go back to so readily. I know, for myself, that I can slip into ego "real" world very easily. That is the hold that ego has on us all.

But when we slow our pace, breathe, and find our source, we see the truth of the matter. That is the spiritual re-wiring that is necessary. It is the realization that the ego does its best to constantly control the situation, or make us feel like we have controlled the situation, in order to "feed." When we recognize this, then we may bless our ego, in gratitude for helping us recognize this, and illuminate it with spirit, making *each* situation something that can be spiritual.

> *We are both imminent and transcendent beings: imminent*
> *in the world of matter as evidenced through our physical*
> *senses, emotions, and thoughts, and transcendent*

> *as the non-material Self that simply witnesses*
> Michael Bernard Beckwith
> *The Answer is You*

One of the most difficult aspects of spiritual existence is letting go of thoughts, no matter how intelligent and logical they may be, and allowing the feelings of joy, love, service, which are the natural state of our spiritual being, to emerge. Those feelings are always there, but become ignored, as the ego attempts to dominate our perspective. We allow our fears to convince us that we need to have control over everything and that we can force this life to bend at our will. Our separatist-self, is a master of illusion in this manner, as we never have true control. The truth is that we can only choose how we experience existence.

> *Let go and let God*
> *Christian Poem*
> *Credited to Lauretta P. Burns*

The hardest part is letting go. When you do, God is obvious. The pull of the ego is a great force, but the hardest part of the battle is recognition. This is the growth... the lesson.

When I work out in the public gym, I see so many people there that watch themselves in the mirror. I do not pretend to know what they are thinking or feeling, but the very act places sole focus on the body capsule, and takes energy away from the spirit.

> *To see spirit, to feel it, you must go inside*
> *by letting go of the outside*

Whenever possible catch yourself when viewing people from the perspective of their looks, or their particular intellectual level or even their personality, which are *all* ego. Remind yourself that the real person is the infinite being within, and do your best to see them this way.

By seeing ourselves as separate, we introduce the concepts of fear, evil, good, bad.

Duality can ONLY exist when we see each other as separate!

So often, people try to beat the "bad" guy, conquer fear and destroy evil because these are energies that the "other person" is using against us. When we see each other all as the same, all as part of the common source, we recognize duality for what it really is, our own egos attempting to perpetuate the non-reality.

> *Evil cannot be conquered via conflict, as the act of conflict only adds power to the illusion, which generates its existence. It can only be resolved by adopting a consciousness of unity rather than separation*
> Owen Waters
> *The Shift: The Revolution in Human Consciousness*

Ego is not something that we must conquer. That would only feed it and make it more prominent. That would make the Pain-Body thrive. Ego is a part of us. We do not want to destroy it, only illuminate it. This is done by spirit, not by battle.

How Do We Get There?

Such experiences repeat themselves until we learn to
ask more skillful, self-revealing questions such as: What
quality must I cultivate to shift this circumstance?
What skills am I being called to develop? What would
life have me do here? What can I learn from this?
Michael Bernard Beckwith
The Answer is You

WHEN I READ THE above quote by Beckwith, I think about something I have alluded to through out this book: Our ultimate purpose. What Deepak Chopra referred to as our Dharma: the purpose for our existence, which is to use our skills to serve each other. In so doing we serve this universe, we serve the connection that we are, we serve our common source.

In order to know your Dharma, you must know your consciousness. By raising your self-awareness, you contribute to the global consciousness and raise the overall power of spirit in such a way as to move all of humanity closer to a "critical mass" of consciousness.

Since I choose to put the majority of my energy to living from a spirit-based direction, the majority of this section is devoted to attaining that from my perspective. I hope that there will be some ideas in here that will resonate with you.

I do not feel that the majority of the people live a primarily ego life... at least not intentionally. I do believe that Americans are exposed to the ego world a thousand times more than the rest of the planet because it keeps people in fear. It keeps people feeling like they must protect themselves and their belongings and promotes separation.

A fearful mind is easy to control. We can be told that our country is threatened, our houses are threatened, our belongings, our families, our lives. Those that live in fear will accept what is being said and ask, what do I need to do to protect myself and stay separated? What products must I purchase, what law must be passed, what must we do to beat the "badness?"

Sometimes, to distract our minds from the fear we identify with our sports teams, and pay people millions of dollars, whose very focus is ego-centered because they shoot a basketball better, hit a ball over a fence, hit another person harder, and so on. At the same time police, nurses, and teachers make near-poverty and lower incomes. We will pay hundreds of dollars to go to a "ball game" or purchase flat screen televisions while there are millions of children in our own communities and billions across the globe that go to bed starving, It is no surprise that there remain large numbers of US citizens focused primarily on an ego existence.

Despite this exposure, the more people I meet, the more that I read about the beauty in this world, the more that I believe that the majority of the people in this world and even in the United States are becoming aware of the superficial ego world and recognizing it for what it is.

Every day I meet people who speak from the heart and live to serve others. People in other countries have so little when it comes to material things, or even food and water, yet there are many surveys indicating that they exist at a higher level of happiness than Americans.

Living a happy and joyful life IS the way to spirit. On a website called inspirationalstories.com, the results of a survey showed that the US ranks 46th in happiness in the world, and the country that ranks the highest: Bangladesh... Bangladesh! One of the poorest countries in the world financially!

> *The shift is the mass awakening of humanity's heart.*
> *This transformation of consciousness, the greatest*
> *one ever recorded, first became apparent in the mid-*
> *1960s and has been building momentum ever since*
> Owen Waters
> *The Shift: The Revolution in Human Consciousness*

The good is out there, and it is in YOU! Go within and then let it out. I believe that there is a powerful change coming. I believe that we are about to reach a critical mass of humans in spirit. Here are some practical things, some actual steps that a person may take. I hope that some of these will be of some value:

Seek joy from within. Joy is not in a new car. That is a feeble attempt to fill emptiness in spirit. Joy is in the moment! Marvel at life and how the events that have occurred have brought you to this point, reading a book on spirituality, written by a high school chemistry teacher. I am awestruck on a daily basis at the events that have lead to this moment. We find this joy by seeking within. It is nearly impossible to seek within while simultaneously receiving external stimulus. Learn to be alone with yourself. No radio, no computer, no paper or pencil, no one else... Alone. When you learn to find joy alone then you bring this limitless flow of joy to all situations, rather than seeking it in others, or in alcohol, or other external sources. This takes practice.

You are a being of pure spiritual joy. As such, you have the ability to touch joy in yourself and when coming in contact with others. Look within at the spiritual observer and bathe yourself in the joy of the true consciousness.

Meditate/pray or perform yoga. There are few activities that a person can do that bring you closer to spirit than meditation or prayer.

> *If you bring forth what is within you, what you bring forth*
> *will save you. If you do not bring forth what is within*
> *you, what you do not bring forth will destroy you*
> Gospel of St. Thomas
> ThinkExist.com

Spirit is not found in words or song... perhaps this is found in the feelings that are elicited from these. Yes you can feel spiritual in listening to music, but to find the true self, you must be still. You come in contact with this when you are quiet and seek in the space between the words. When we are quiet, we see what is already there, we hear spirit, we live it, feel it.

Spirit is always there we just don't take the time to be silent and quiet our minds. There is far too much mind-chatter in our lives. There is always something to distract our focus and take our attention back to this egoic reality. We must get away from the computer, the ipads, the ipods, the twitter, and find the spirit that exists in the silence.

I have often felt that this is the reason that so many sacred works of art, music, poetry and the like seem to have taken place hundreds and even thousands of years ago in human history. There were so few distractions for humans then that they could listen to the quiet and be more contemplative.

In these quiet moments of meditation ask what is your highest purpose. Listen to the mind inside your heart. This is the subtle voice that has always been there but we never seem to be able to give it enough time to just sit and listen. It is the feeling that we need to sit still but there are always "good" reasons not to.

The spirit within knows what your highest purpose is. It is not about making money, although you might. It is not about influencing massive amounts of people, although that is possible. It will always have something to do with service to others, so listen and have the faith in yourself that whatever it is, it is *your* unique gift to the world. Trust what you receive as your gift. It will be a special talent or motivation and will always be in service. Follow it and it will take you to wondrous new adventures.

Meditation is being present to the spirit in the silence. Yoga is being present to the true body of light that is your spirit as well. Find peace and joy in these and they will lead you to the common source.

Within all of us, there is the enlightened spirit, but it will not burst out of us, like a door-to-door salesman. It only comes when you invite it out through self-illumination, and this is found in the silence within.

Listen to the little voice and then act in a positive manner. Now that you have asked the question, and meditated to seek the answer, you must listen for the response and then act on it. Be a yes-man or woman.

Have you ever gone through a day or a week, or a year, when you continually see or hear subtle reminders or indicators of a particular activity? These may be acts, like writing a book, or feelings, like love one another, or trying out new experiences, such as changing a job to something completely different?

These are inspirations. These are your gifts attempting to rise to the surface, if only you will recognize them. These are your spiritual connection attempting to gain your attention in a subtle manner.

> *Inspiration: The immediate influence of God or a god*
> *online etymology dictionary*

These are messages from God, but you must pay attention. And then take action. These subtle messages can come from coincidental billboards, or a book that falls off a bookshelf at the library, or come up in conversations. Sometimes these latent messages slip past our conscious mind until later contemplation, such as meditation, brings them to light. Other times, they make you pause in the moment to wonder, "What if?" This is the spirit speaking to you.

This happened to me while living at my father's house as his caregiver. I was in a very trying time in my life and my heart ached. In the very room that I had been staying for four years at that point, I noticed a book that stood out of the bookcase in the room. I had seen this bookcase every day for that four-year period, but this book almost jumped off the shelf. It seemed to stand out over all of the other books on the shelf, yet for no apparent reason. The book, <u>Care of the Soul</u>, By Thomas Moore, was exactly what I needed to read at the time. I found myself reading paragraphs over several times and underlining sentences. This was a book that my mother had purchased several years earlier, and had remained on the shelf since her passing. I have no doubt that the spiritual connection with her made it clear that this book would help me move forward. The point was that it was subtle... Spirit always is, and it brought great joy to me... again, an indication that this was a gift of loving spirit.

Each time we have a choice to respond to these subtleties or to ignore them. If we ignore them long enough they tend to fade into the background of life and its "busy-ness." if we act on them, we will, not *may*... *will*, find new doors and new directions in life that will stimulate us in so many ways, that we will wonder how we went so long with out them. They will open new spiritual doors, and we will make new connections. This is never a bad thing.

Following inspiration will continue to inspire further. Following these gentle nudges will always evolve us and bring us closer to source. I encourage everyone to take action on these. This is God-source trying to get our attention. Remember that Source is more like a whisper than a shout… only the ego shouts. You would do well to ignore the screams of ego and listen to the whisper of spirit and to take action. Be a yes-man (or yes-woman)!

Live a life of forgiveness, discovery and gratitude. Three of the greatest lessons that we can learn in order to evolve are to forgive, discover with open hearts, and be grateful for the gifts of life.

> *We accept that ultimately all things are working together*
> *for our good, that they are invitations to more deeply*
> *participate in our ever-evolving consciousness*
> Michael Bernard Beckwith
> *The Answer is You*

After reading this statement from Michael Beckwith, how can we not be grateful for everything in our lives?

Gratitude, from the Latin, gratus, means thankful and pleasing. Being grateful will take us to new levels of growth. If we can be thankful for everything in life… Not just what we like but everything, we can release the stress of anger and resentment from the past, as well as the stress and worry of the future. In this way we are totally present. All too often people are not grateful until things that they perceive to be good, "happen" to them. If only they would realize that being grateful *is* the "good" in their lives and will attract more of the positive energy flow to their lives. Everything that has occurred to this moment has brought you to this point. Be glad.

Forgiveness from the Latin, perdonare, or to pardon, is so self-empowering. In this situation, it does not mean to seek out another and tell them that you forgive them, which is actually more ego-centric than spiritual, but rather to release or pardon actions or events in your mind, in order to bring all situations back to spirit.

I learned a technique of forgiveness from my friend and life mentor, Walter Parish. It is empowering and helps you to reflect and refocus on the spirit. Start by first identifying what you perceive another person has done "to" you. In your feeling place, make the statement, "I forgive you for (transgression), I give you permission to forgive me, and I forgive myself for any pain I may have caused myself." After this, find the lesson to be learned from the situation, and be grateful for this lesson. Repeat this process as many times as necessary to really start to feel an easing of tension in the solar plexus. It will come with practice and belief.

In forgiveness we open our hearts to discover what the lesson may be. By releasing the ego-part of a situation our spiritual eyes are opened and we may be awakened to the actual lesson.

As I reflect on my life, I am convinced that my greatest teachers were those that challenged me to forgive them in my heart to bring me to seek and to be grateful for what they have taught me about myself. For the things that we need to forgive others for, are the things that we need to forgive ourselves for. That is a lesson that is truly worthy of being grateful.

> *Through discovery and marveling in the circumstances*
> *of our present life we grow closer to our true purpose.*
> *When we refuse to let go, refuse to release the past*
> *we lose sight of the vast wave of possibilities that may*
> *be available to us in these new circumstances.*

Keep a watchful eye for the blessing in every situation. There is discovery in spirit as we release our egoic trappings, and are grateful for events and people in our lives… look for the new direction that you will be lead.

The combination of forgiveness, discovery and gratitude is a powerful way to stay present and stay in spirit. In doing this you will make room for your true inner happiness, and by doing so you will bring heaven and earth together. Live your life by releasing others of the way that they have "offended" your ego and be grateful for the gift that they have been and the lessons that they have taught you.

Every day, scare yourself. Remember that fear is generated in the ego, so when you face fears, you bring your ego into the light and illuminate it for what it really is... *false self.* When you illuminate ego you release that part of your ego that you have been reluctant to let go of.

> *Do one thing every day that scares you*
> Eleanor Roosevelt

These may be any type of acts or feelings. I am not advocating that you jump out of airplanes or hang-glide, unless you are motivated to do so. Deep down, there is a part of you that is afraid to do something, express something, open yourself up to something. You fill in the blank.

For a great many years, I had not opened myself up to love from a significant other. I thought that I had but there was a part of me that always sabotaged that, by finding flaws in the other, or coming on too strong. As I have moved forward in my learning, I realized that it was not that the other person had flaws... It was because I was not in self-awareness. As a result I had a false fear of being in a situation that I would not be able to control.

When I realized that all things in my life are brought to me to help me evolve to my greatest spiritual awareness, I also realized that even in my darkest moments, my only responsibility is to embrace that moment and know that it will take me somewhere new. It took me inside to find my true self. Then the right person entered my life.

As a result, I have now opened my heart to true love of a significant other and have met a very special woman whom I love deeply, and whom I am engaged to. There were times during the early part of our relationship that I felt the old fear knocking on my spiritual door. The difference was that I recognized it for what it was... False. I opened up to illuminate the fear rather than running from it. As a result, I am now happier and more at peace with Angie in my life. I know now that she was brought into my life for a reason, and only at the moment that I was ready to accept her magnificent love.

> *Being on the third floor does not mean that you will no*
> *longer have the natural, normal, emotional responses*
> *to life and its often nerve-wracking situations. What it*
> *means is that you will quickly recover from an emotional*
> *upheaval because you will apply love to the situation*
> Iyanla Vanzant
> *In the Meantime: Finding yourself and the Love You want*

We have become the support that each needs in our lives. She is such a beautiful spirit, and I feel like she was absolutely placed in my life strictly for me. She is joyful, and loving. The other night, she told me that she felt my father's presence with her. She never met my dad in physical form but felt that he was there advising her. I know that we are right for each other but never would have known that had I not brought my fear to light.

There is a difference between fear and good sense. It is not good sense to walk down the middle of a busy freeway at night. Facing fears and bringing them to light is not about being a daredevil. It is about the deep ceded fear that has controlled you and kept you from realizing your fullest spiritual potential.

What are the things that you are afraid of, that keep coming up in your life? They keep popping up because the spirit is giving you a subtle opportunity to release that part of the false self and illuminate your spirit. Are you willing to see the light or will you continue to hide in the darkness of your ego?

How do we get to certain points in our lives? Where we are at present is based on our willingness to either run away from or welcome our fears, to surrender to them, then shining the light of truth on them.

This is not about conquering. We are not vanquishing some dark specter in the deep recesses of our subconscious. Our subconscious is a manifestation of the way that we look at others and ourselves. Do you seek ego or do you seek spirit?

This is about embracing. Remember that everything that comes into your life is there to offer you an opportunity to evolve in one direction or another. Embrace it and follow your heart. Allow the beauty of life to lead you to spirit.

Savor each moment. As I sit in my car in front of the school at which I teach, it is October. I look at the beauty of the fall colors; I experience the crisp cool air and notice the silence around me. I am awestruck by the beauty brought to me in his moment. I lean over to type and then look back up at the trees and am inspired. This is no fluke of a cosmic coincidence. The beauty of which I savor in this moment was brought to me, and I to it, so that it may be appreciated, right here... right now. What is real beauty?

> *For the soul, then, beauty is not defined as*
> *pleasantness of form but rather as the quality in*
> *things that invites absorption and contemplation*
> Thomas Moore, Care of the Soul

How often do you take the time to be present to the marvel of nature, the wonder of your body as it coordinates millions of chemical reactions at once? How often do you reflect on the closeness of a friend, or for that matter anyone. When was the last time that you marveled at the ability of a blade of grass to grow and convert solar energy to chemical energy so that we can consume it?

As a chemistry teacher, I still marvel at the design of water. It amazes me that because of two pairs of lone electrons around the oxygen atom, that water is a bent molecule, thus allowing it to be a partially polar molecule. This makes water a liquid at room temperature. The very fact that it is a partially polar liquid allows it to be the medium that all chemical reactions in our body take place. So the location of four electrons around an oxygen atom is what allows for life, as we understand it on this planet! That is *not* an accident. The more I learn about science, the more I am certain that all life, every aspect of it is completely divine.

Every moment of every day, there are wonders, and when you are present to the moment, problems cease to exist… if only for that moment. There is no future stress, and there is no past regret. There is only the miracle of now. Are you present to this miracle?

Spend quality time with loved ones. Spending time with people that you love, particularly, a person that you have not been able to spend much time with recently is so fulfilling.

Reach out to friends from across the country. Plan a vacation to see family members or friends. Reconnect the bonds that have lain dormant but were always there. It never fails that whenever I spend time talking to old friends on the phone or at their house, we end up talking deeply and sharing and gaining perspective. I always leave more enriched.

Before my dad passed over last June, I called him every Sunday from Boise to Tucson. Our conversations were rarely long, but I think we always wanted them to be. We would talk about the University of Arizona basketball or football teams, then the conversation would swing to what was happening in Boise, and how teaching was going. At the end of the conversation we always finished with a true expression of how we felt. I would say, "I love you dad," and he would say, "I love you son." I truly miss that Sunday conversation and always finishing with a proclamation of our love for each other. I know that he is around me all the time, but I will always miss that time that we spent together. I cherish each of those moments and am so happy that I have those memories to draw from.

Now I spend that quality time with the woman I love, and we make sure that we have time alone together, just holding each other and being together. What else could we need in that moment?

Connect with the unconditional love of a pet. It may sound a bit unconventional for a spiritual book, but animals express the purest form of unconditional love. In the same vein as reconnecting with friends or family members, realize that many of us have pets that love us unconditionally and only seek to make us happy. Time and again, I am amazed at the way that family pets are treated. I am not talking about animal abuse, where sociopathic humans, mutilate, neglect or battle their pets against others. That is an entirely different level of pathological egocentrism.

I am only speaking of the family dog that is brought home and put in a cage all year long, to live a life in a ten foot by ten foot area in all forms of weather, or worse chained to a post in the back yard, only experiencing human contact when someone feeds them or brings water to them. They long to interact with us, to protect us, to share joy with us. If you spend enough time with pets, you can see the joy, the sadness, and the love.

In the time that I have spent with my dog, now fourteen years old, I have found her to be such a gentle and caring being. She misses me when I am gone and always expresses her joy when I finally arrive home from twelve-hour days of teaching. She loves all spirits unconditionally and her gentle, kind ways are a reflection of that. I rescued my half pit-bull from the humane society and she has been grateful ever since.

If only we could emulate the ability of animals to live in the present moment. They are the ultimate in doing this. As soon as some event is over, they have forgotten it. They never stress over the future regardless of what has taken place in the past. They live in the moment. When you spend enough time with them, you "get" that. Spend time with your pets and see if you can learn the spiritual lesson that they have to teach you.

Spiritual Worship. Whatever level of spiritual worship you are at, dig deep into it. Join the fellowship of joyful spirit.

> *While you may find a level of ritualistic routine for comfort, <u>it is only through depth that you will find spirit.</u>*

Everyone possesses various levels of religious perspective. As stated earlier, it is not in the words but the feeling space between the words that matter. Religious rituals do not have the depth of spirit. These are only a type of framework to help us seek depth. There are many such frameworks.

The rituals may get you to attend your "church" but it is the spiritual depth in which you will find true source, joy and happiness. This can be found in the sharing of the joyful fellowship in a religious ceremony as well as the deep feelings that can be invoked during a beautiful experience in nature. Please look past the ceremony and see the spirit that inspired the ceremony. Whenever I attend a religious service, I close my eyes while a "sermon" is in progress and attempt to feel the spirit, which motivated the words.

Whether you attend a religious ceremony in a building or find your "church" to be in the woods or on a mountaintop, the key is to find the beautiful spirit place deep within yourself that you can share with others. This is the place in which the common source is found.

Don't Judge. If there is any one aspect of humans that projects self-reflection of the fears and darkness of the ego-consciousness, it is judgment of others. It is everywhere. We judge what people look like, what they wear, how they act, the way that they drive, and on and on. We then project this to be what is called being a "good" person or a "bad" person. Are there actions that are appropriate and inappropriate for the spiritual evolution of humanity? Yes, absolutely. Does that make a person "good" or "bad?" Not in my opinion.

There are only those of Source that are controlled by ego fears or recognize and illuminate the ego with spiritual love. Actions are the result of these views. The bible addresses judgment several times. Buddhists believe that the judgment of others says more about the person making the judgment rather than those being judged.

> *Judge not that ye not be judged*
> Matthew 7:1

Judgment can only lead to more ego-based responses. Instead, simply try to see that another spirit is going through their own lessons. They may be feeling pain or anger, or fear. Offer help, assistance, love, caring, counsel. Be there for them without forcing your ideas on them. When the time is appropriate, they will be grateful for your acceptance. You will have made a real difference in another person's life.

Love. In all aspects of life, when it seems so difficult to respond to a situation appropriately, or to handle something without fear, turn your energy into love. Our ego has a strong hold over our emotional response to people and events. It amazes me how automatically we respond with fear or anger to feed our ego-selves.

> *Love is always more powerful than fear. I truly believe*
> *that love is the most powerful energy in the universe*

185

There is nothing that cannot be transmuted by the loving energy that is God, or Ra, or Allah, or whatever name that we have given our source. By feeding a situation with the deep ceded love that is our source, we can turn everyday events into moments of greatness. Examples of this are everywhere and in everything. The following is a common, if not silly example of such a situation.

Every morning after my workouts, I find it relaxing to sit in the hot tub at the club. Not only this, but there is a corner of the hot tub which is particularly pleasant, with just the right power jets and angles of hot water streaming to my lower back. I find it most relaxing. One morning, while getting ready for my hot tub routine, as I was walking towards the ladder to lower my body into the steaming water, a man emerged from the sauna and stepped in front of me. He then proceeded to walk down the ladder into the hot tub. Further, he then went to the same location that I normally do, in the hot tub. I ended up moving to another side of the hot tub where the jets are not as strong. I sat in this unfamiliar corner and stewed about how this man had not only cut me off but also had the gall to then take *my* spot. He was clearly new and did not know that was my place. As I sat for a minute or two, I realized how silly this was, and changed my perspective. Instead of viewing this innocent man as an egotistic, inconsiderate, lug, I changed over to love. I saw this man as connected directly to me and as having a common source. I remained in the tub a few more minutes, and decided to depart. As I did, I made it a point to look at his eyes. I looked with the understanding and recognition as a brother would to another brother, and smiled. We had connected instead of conflicting.

This is just one example of transforming situations with love. I felt better and there was no source of egocentric stress. We can all transform each moment and event in our lives the same way, simply by awareness and illumination. Once again I point to the scripture that God is Love.

Whoever does not love, does not know
God, because God is Love
1 John 4:8

I believe that you may empower your spirit in ways that ego-centered people cannot comprehend, simply by using the highest energy possible in all situations.

Further if you see through the eyes of love, then you see through the eyes of God. In doing so, you can always see the good in all situations. When you find the good, you are tying everything back to source. It is not easy when things get difficult but is always rewarding, and it always brings you back to your purpose.

Why Bother? My Wish For Us All

The growing realization that our continued
survival depends upon dispelling the illusion
that we are separate from one another...
Michele Bernard Beckwith
Spiritual Liberation

As I STATED EARLY in this book, these are just observations. Why should we bother to spend time examining this? The quote by Beckwith above is the ultimate response to this question.

So when is it time to change the way that we live? When do we see ourselves in the REAL world?

The world of spirit is ever present in our lives. It is there
but does not force itself into our view. It presents itself
to us constantly. The question is, do you see it? Can
you quiet your ego-centered mind chatter long enough
to hear your true-self speaking to you in love?

It is not a world of conditioned responses to actions giving "good" and "bad," judging "right" and "wrong." It is not a world of dualistic thinking. It is something that can be applied to everyday thinking and when it is, always helps us arrive at the highest order of spirit in every situation. It is not exclusive of the material world.

Christian religions offer baptism as a means to bring recognition for people moving from darkness into light. There are many metaphorical examples of baptism into light in the bible. The first reference, although the word baptism is not used, there is still the use of water as a metaphor to move from darkness and into the light of holy spirit, is found in Genesis.

> *In the beginning God created the heavens and the earth. Now*
> *the earth was formless and empty, darkness was over the*
> *surface of the deep, and the Spirit of God was hovering over the*
> *waters. And God said, "Let there be light," and there was light.*
> Genesis 1:1-3

As you read this passage it may be a bit of a stretch to draw the correlation between "formless and empty" to mean the ego, however the obvious correlation of moving from darkness as the "Spirit of God was hovering over the waters" to light is undeniably tied to the concept of baptism.

In the Catholic Church, baptism is the first sacrament because it is the door of the spiritual life. This is the door that we must open to illuminate our ego world with spirit. Through this approach, anyone turning inward to spirit and passing through the door of illumination is being baptized.

While attending service I recall a priest of an Episcopal faith expressing that the light of the holy spirit was sewn into each of us and it was our responsibility to recognize the particular gift of the holy spirit. I was struck by his use of the term sewn several times during the sermon. This left me with a true sense of cultivating a seed of something that was placed there by Source. In recognizing it, we would see it grow and its purpose was always in service and always through Love. This means that it is always in service to each other because we are all connected to source.

> *Who looks outside, dreams; who looks within, awakens*
> *Carl Jung*

We all have a special light of Source in us. It may be called Dharma, or Holy Spirit. It is our purpose. It is our service to each other in recognition of our common connection. If we do not recognize it, then, like seeds that fall on to rock, they will not blossom. They will remain dormant, and we will remain in our ego world.

In Christianity the baptism is a reminder that we are spiritual in nature and it is used, in my opinion, as a means to ceremoniously move away from ego and seek the common spiritual self. This is the light that is "sewn" into our being. Although most Christian baptisms occur early in life, there is the ever-present reminder that we were baptized with the presence of Holy water near the entrance of churches. This reminder is there to gently nudge us toward seeking our spiritual awareness.

> *Jesus says: Know what is before your face, and*
> *what is hidden from you will be revealed to you.*
> *For nothing hidden will fail to be revealed*
> Gospel of Thomas Saying 5

It is a blending of spirit source into a weave of a harmonistic approach to the physical moment. It is utilizing the physical moment that we have here to realize our spiritual plane, and to love this existence, just for its very existence. In short, it is Heaven on earth.

> *How many years can some people exist, before they're*
> *allowed to be free... Yes and how many ears must one man*
> *have before he can hear people cry? The answer, my friend,*
> *is blowin' in the wind. The answer is blowin' in the wind*
> Bob Dylan
> Folk Singer

I do not pretend to understand Bob Dylan's perspective at the time that he wrote the lyrics to <u>Blowin in the Wind</u>, but I think we must ask the question, how much more? How much longer do we continue to deny our spiritual self and remain *only* in the ego "real" world?

We know deep down that we are not separate beings, no matter how different we may physically look. We know that we all have the same Source and that when we look at each other using "spirit glasses" there is no doubt what we really see. We also know that it is appropriate to help those that need us, to treat others with kindness, to serve, to love, to enjoy life. Yet somehow we continue to simply accept the ego-world completely, and to participate in it. The ego has a strong grip, but it can be loved into spirit, by illumination.

Deep inside we know that all life is sacred, yet we justify killing. We can feel the importance for living in the present, but we continue to fret the future and regret the past. We have the distinct sense that this world is better when we raise others up, and see this as a world of abundance, but we continue to compete for "our" share of the pie. This is the ego world whose foundation is described in the book, <u>The Origin of the Species,</u> by Charles Darwin, in which he outlined the concept of survival of the fittest.

It is time for a paradigm shift in the way that look at ourselves and each other. This is far from a new idea.

Jesus said: As you give, so shall you receive
Luke 6:38

People living in spirit realize that this was not just about caring for others but that this was Jesus' way of keeping the gifts of this life flowing through our existence. This was about abundance of spirit.

So how much longer before we look inside for God, before we see God in others, before we realize that we are all the same and all created in the image of love. When do we see that the ego world is constant film-loop of pain, misery, fear, competition, and anger and will continue to be so until we illuminate it with the light of Source... Love.

> *Darkness cannot drive out darkness; only light can do*
> *that. Hate cannot drive out hate; only love can do that*
> *Dr. Martin Luther King Jr.*

Love is always the answer to fear and ego. When we can all move in the direction of spirit, war will not be necessary because we will love *for* each other instead of fear against each other. One of the best quotes I have ever read truly puts our existence into perspective and why we should bother to look for spirit in ourselves, in others and in the circumstances of life constantly:

> *You don't have a soul. You are a soul. You have a body*
> *C.S. Lewis*

Anyone who has ever been with someone at his or her "deathbed" understands this statement. When my mother passed over in December of 2001, I was at her bedside in the intensive care unit. After her body ceased to function there was an initial, painful feeling of loss, I was alone in the room until the rest of the family arrived. It was abundantly clear that this was simply a capsule that held my mothers true self. The Ghost in the Machine had departed. Her true self had simply changed planes of existence. I do not need physical evidence of this... I KNOW IT!

Why bother??!! We bother because we are the same. Because we are not here simply to discover our gifts, and our bliss, but to share those with our spiritual brothers and sisters, and to help others discover and share theirs. It completes our physical incarnation. Underline: <u>What other purpose can we possibly have?</u>

> *... we are spiritual beings who have taken physical form*
> *<u>to fulfill a purpose.</u> When we blend this unique talent*
> *with service to others, we experience the ecstasy and*
> *exaltation of our spirit. This is the goal of all goals*
> *Deepak Chopra referring to our Dharma*
> *The Seven Spiritual Laws of Success*

Deep down, we know that love is the answer, that God, or Allah, Ra, Source, is a benevolent, loving, caring energy; the most powerful energy of the universe. Source is not judgmental. Source is not an old man sitting on a cloud with a scorecard keeping track of our "good and bad" deeds.

Source is inspiration, idealistic, caring, nurturing of *all*. It is the energy that unifies everything, the spirit we seek in the seldom-quiet moments of our lives. It appears momentarily, like a blind spot in our vision. With one considerable difference: we can choose to see this, to live it, to be it, because we *are* this source... all of us. It is time!

> *The created universe is waiting with eager*
> *expectation for Gods sons to be revealed*
> *Romans 8:19*

Remember that darkness is always illuminated by light and that darkness cannot overtake light. In the same way fear and ego are always illuminated by love.

> *Love is always a higher power, and is always*
> *the way that makes you feel good.*

From the Latin *Inspirare*, meaning to breathe, inspiration brings us life, harmony and joy. Divine inspiration was the reason and the way that I wrote this book.

I listened and noticed the little nudges that kept appearing in my life to sit down and do this. I am inspired with ideas and most importantly; I listened to this inspiration and acted on it. If sharing this discovery helps one other person illuminate their spirit, then it has been worth every bit of effort, research and time.

When fear-driven thoughts appear, we have a built in mechanism to expose them for the ego-driven thoughts that they are: they make us feel bad. We can tell when thoughts are of ego because they make us feel, at the least, uneasy, and at worst may even lead to panic attacks. These may be scary until we see them for what they are... Fear.

When we bring fear out into light, it is illuminated and we will have learned a lesson. This happens *every* time as long as we recognize it. Our bodies are tied to the true self and respond in a way that helps signal if ideas are appropriate for us and for the entire universe. We just need to pay attention. David Hawkins actually quantified this in his book, <u>Power Versus Force</u>, which I have alluded to several times in this book already.

Writing this book is my soul work. It is the expression of the feeling place of my heart. The words may be mine, but the intention of the words, come from the Loving universe and they belong to all. It is time!

> *What is being born is a new consciousness and, as*
> *its inevitable reflection, a new world. This is also*
> *foretold in the New Testament book of Revelation:*
> *" Then I saw a new heaven and a new earth, for the*
> *first heaven and the first earth had passed away."*
> *Eckhart Tolle, Revelation 21:1*
> *The Power of Now*

As a result of processing the thoughts that have gone into this book, I have noticed a change in myself along the amazing journey. I find myself being more alert to the people around me. I find myself more open, caring, and compassionate. I notice that when I first respond to situations with anger, and fear, I step back and see the other person as God, always connected to me. It has changed the way that I travel through this life. On this journey, I have been transformed into the person that truly reflects the spirit.

Read the words to the song Shine Like It Does. As I reflect on the music that I have enjoyed most, I feel like I may have missed the message the first time, but in this song, I have finally "heard" the enlightenment. It has touched me and it made me realize that this new world has been emerging for many years.

This is the power, since time began, every single hour,
that we have known, and from each moment, all
hat is left, sleep of the innocent, just one desire

Shine like it does
Into every heart
Shine like it does
And if you are looking
You will find it

This is the story, since time began, there will
come a day, when we will know
Band: INXS
Shine Like it Does

Now, again, I do not pretend to know what INXS was intending when they sang these lyrics, but they are steeped with spiritual awareness.

I feel like it is a reminder that we must seek our true self, our ultimate observer, and note the Dharma from within. In seeking we will find it.

It is our nature to be curious, to seek, to wonder about existence. Many experts use very vague language in answering the question, "What is the meaning of life?"

There is nothing vague about the way that Michael Bernard Beckwith addresses this topic. In his discussion on the three turns of the key I believe he reveals the way to our Dharma. Below is a discussion of these three turns of the key from his book, <u>Spiritual Liberation</u>:

> *With Three Turns of a Key*
> *In this passage the first turn is asking the question, "Who am I?" Beckwith states "You can not be your Authentic Self without becoming intimate with your true nature."*

The first turn of the key, "Who am I?"

Have you ever really looked inside to see the real you? I refer back to the CS Lewis quote, that we are souls. Throughout our lives we are taught by society that we are our bodies, our minds, or level of academic achievement, our job status, our bank account.

On a PBS special, Wayne Dyer spoke about this very thing. He referenced the fact that we came from no-where to now-here and we will return to no-where.

Our egos view and project our identities as our intelligence, or our physique, or our accomplishments. These are all aspects of the now-here but will soon be no-where. This is why it is so valuable to our purpose to relate to our true selves and the true nature of all life. When we do this we see that we are not individual but a part of the whole.

The second turn is asking the question, "Why am I here?"

All of us have a need to know what our true purpose is. This is not about occupations, or social roles, like parent. This is a reference to our purpose from the perspective of the soul. What is the purpose for our incarnation? When we know the purpose, we can take steps to express this. When we come to this understanding we can use our occupation or social standing as a *vehicle to assist* us in accomplishing our true purpose.

However, it is not *necessary* to use our position, as we can serve everywhere we go and in everyway that we interact with people. As referred to earlier by Deepak Chopra, our purpose is our Dharma. It is the use of our gifts to serve this universe in its entirety.

I truly believe that my purpose is to bring joy and help others seek self-awareness. I can use my teaching position to accomplish this but I can also do this by a smile at a stranger at the gym, or holding the door for someone at the coffee shop. An interesting by-product of this is that in expressing joy to others, I receive it at the same time. This is the law of abundance and circulation at work.

I use my gifts of relate-ability, love, caring, compassion, empathy, and spiritual happiness to serve those around me. A gentle smile and gaze deep into the eyes of another can warm them as well as myself in a spiritual recognition and reassurance that we are actually here for each other. In this way, I hope to teach them that they can let their ego-guard down and find the true self that we all share.

The third turn of the key is the use of spiritual discipline such as meditation.

Meditation is paramount in answering the first two questions and then learning the most appropriate manner to express them. Through meditation we reunite with the authentic self, and the source that is us. There is no better way to re-center and illuminate that which we see as challenges in our ego lives.

Just asking the questions is paramount to the success of our movement to self-awareness. As a teacher, I know that when my students ask questions, then we are half way, or farther, to getting the understanding we seek.

At every age and stage of development, questions energize our thinking and expand our awareness… While our brain is wired to question, the good news is that our inherent intelligence and intuition are wired to answer. Within every question is an answer endeavoring to reveal itself, which is another way of saying the answer, is in the question
Michael Bernard Beckwith
The Answer is You

Why should we seek spiritual awareness? Why should we seek our reality, our real self, and our real source?

After teaching high school for over twenty years, I feel aware that the students have taught me far more about what is real than I have taught them about science. They have not been exposed to the ego world as long as adults have, and their spirit is obvious. In their short time as incarnate beings, they are still focused on the development of their identity and have not yet learned to identify with the fear-based world that surrounds us with a constant influx of controlling and superficial energy.

In most cases they are not even aware of their own, spiritual identity. It is obvious, that their real identity is far deeper than they are willing to look at this point in their development and yet is easier to tap into from my perspective as the joyful observer.

I have watched many of them in emotional pain because they cannot see who they really are, and the ego world in which they must interact is painful and fearful. The lack of spiritual awareness is evidenced in the way that they abuse drugs, alcohol, self-deprecate, and even in the way that they escape into video games. Their pain is obvious and remains such until there is a conscious decision made to move away from the mind-chatter, and the mind-numbing distractions, and move toward self-awareness. As adults going through our own journey we can help them by being their spiritual mirrors.

On a large scale, this world toils in war, famine, poverty, injustice, persecution and the like because we don't know who we really are and the ego has a death grip on our true self with no intention of letting go. Our ego holds us tightly because it is driven by fear, and only in loving the object of fear can we transform it to spirit.

People constantly seem to be seeking, searching for the "Golden Fleece." Trying to find something to fill what they perceive as gaps. Some try to fill it with material items, or false love, some with anger, and others with alcohol, drugs, or other addictions. These only mask the emptiness that we perceive.

> *The truth is that there is no emptiness. There is only our*
> *lack of willingness or ability to seek the true self, because*
> *in doing so, we must illuminate the ego-world, and our*
> *egos will resist this in every way shape and form.*

Our egos will use tricks and fear. Fear forces us to view events emotionally like being offended, or having a strong, dualistic sense of right and wrong, and a sense of insecurity, and physical pain. The ego will engorge itself in words and thoughts such as terrorist, warfare, and national symbols, even the American flag. The ego-based entity can utilize religion as a means to shield itself from others and remain cocooned in its "safe-house."

The commercial world is our ego-world magnified a thousand times, because it plays right back into the cycle by using fears and other emotions to sell and perpetuate the system of materialism. It teaches us that we must work more than we should, love less than we ought, serve only ourselves, buy more than we can afford, and then start all over the next day.

The ego sits in the shadows afraid to stop this cycle and all-too-often we simply accept what is happening without seeking truth, without bringing ego to light. A great many people sense that there must be a better way but have no idea where to turn to find it. If only they knew that the answer is within.

We must make a conscious choice to illuminate. It is time for us to evolve to our true existence in this real world. We have toiled long enough. It is time for the next step in our evolution. It is not a new technology, nor weapon. It is the realization of what we are.

Every great human event is preceded by a challenge or challenges, whether that is a single human or all of humanity; the light only opens up through the darkness. It is the light that we can see in the distance. We are at a precipice of humanity. It is *now*.

The "new Heaven, " and the "new earth" are upon us, and all we need do is see them. There is a great deal of emotional and physical, and psychological pain caused by our false self.

On this precipice we have the choice to continue the way we always have or to look inside. We cannot wait for someone else to change us. We must do it for ourselves, for each other. If we do, then everyday will truly be a gift.

"Be the change that you wish to see"
Mohandas Karamchand Gandhi

It is time for the real world to stand up... Will you?

Our ON-GOING Spiritual Journey

HAVE YOU EVER FELT like there must be more to life than what we experience on a daily basis? Deep down, haven't you felt that there was another level to you and to everyone else, besides the daily, forceful pushing and pulling of the ego "real" world? Does it feel as though your euphoric vision is just out of reach and that if you could just catch a glimpse of it that you would *know* that this was what you were meant to be?

When I first started thinking about writing a book about spirituality and life, my ego kept telling me that I could not do it, that I did not have the credentials, nor the ability. It told me that no one would listen or care.

As life continued to unfold, small, subtle hints, continued to appear. They were gentle nudges, telling me to just keep going. To follow what I wanted to do; that what I felt was appropriate. These were the quietest inspirations in the back of my mind, and despite my nay-saying ego, I started to take notes as ideas continued to trickle in. Then an amazing transition took place. The trickle turned into a stream, and then a river, and before I knew what was really gong on, my mind began to get flooded with ideas. Where were these coming from? I could not seem to write things down fast enough. No sooner had I completed jotting down one idea, than another three ideas came charging in. It truly felt like I had been holding these back or covering them up for years, but finally listened to the small whispers that were telling me to express myself... that it would somehow help others, and it would work out.

Growing up, I felt as though I was special; that I was destined for some sort of greatness, as all children do because their egos tell them they are. The truth is, that we are all destined for greatness, but fears shut down those ideas in the name of "common sense." Perhaps I was actually still closely linked with my spiritual self but psychology tells us that this is simply a phase in the development of the adolescent brain.

As I reflect on that time, I realize now that I was special; that I *did* have something to offer. This is not meant in an egocentric manner. The more I researched, and contemplated, I now realize that we *all* have a special Dharma to offer this world.

I really began this book as a sort of self-therapy, but it has morphed into a desire to help others. Surely, there are others who may read some small passage that has been written or quote collected in just the right combination as to resonate in someone else's life.

This journey has taken my entire life, but there are peculiar sequences of events that have occurred, which at the time, I had no idea why they were taking place. As I reflect back on them now, I see clearly that they had to occur in this very specific sequence and are continuing to unfold in my life.

In 1991 I read my first spiritual book recommended to me by a Northern Arizona University campus therapist. The book was, Love Is Letting Go Of Fear, by Gerald G. Jampolsky. This was a common sense book about love and fear. This started me thinking about life and particularly people, in a different manner. My processing was very psychology-based. I really did not relate it to spirituality.

I started working at a residential juvenile treatment program that year and tried to apply what I had learned from the book with some of the clients. The results were very mixed, but I like to think that it had some type of impact years later. While I was working full time there, I had been doing my student teaching and began teaching.

I began my first years of teaching, and also began coaching sports. I coached softball, basketball and football. Over time this took a physical toll on my body and I began to receive treatment from a wonderful chiropractor by the name of Ted Winchester in 1996. He worked with aspects other than spinal manipulations. His approach was more of the body, mind, and spirit. It was a very holistic approach and started me thinking about the way that spirit, emotions, and bodies are tied together. Through Ted's recommendations, I started reading more spiritual books.

As I continued to read more and more, I soaked up the lessons but still saw the spiritual aspects and the science as separate. I assumed that Ted was performing some parlor trick when he tested me using a concept that I now know to be applied kinesiology. I did not draw the line of connection between spirit and science at that time. Along came Walter Parish

Walter Parish at Parish Chiropractic in Tucson started to explain the lines of connection and he suggested that I buy and read a book called Dynamic Health by Dr. Ted Morter. This book explained the correlation of the energy field based on scientific understanding. NOW we were talking my language.

At the same time a level of synchronicity was unfolding in my life because I met Father Jamie Conrad. He was an Episcopal priest who talked about quantum physics in his sermons. He would make statements that did not seem like they should be coming from a priest. These ideas along with the others lead me in a new direction.

Back to Walter Parish. He did not practice traditional chiropractic manipulations at all. He simply entered your energy field to see if he could help you identify what was disrupting things.

He used a combination of applied kinesiology and contact points, that in my opinion, are closely aligned with the bodies meridians to help your muscles and body systems relax and function as they should.

Both Walter and Jamie helped me through very difficult times, such as the passing of my brother and mom.

It was about this time that I saw a movie called, <u>What the Bleep Do We Know?</u>

This movie finally put the spirit and the science together for me. At this point, everything in my life had either been cognitive, such as chemistry and biology, or physical, such as coaching. This movie used quantum physics to associate thoughts, feelings, biochemistry and the quantum world in a scientific and methodical way. It tied hundreds of case studies and brought together experts in a great many scientific fields to illustrate the point that science is not exclusive of spirituality. This was exactly what I needed! I was a scientist, but deep down, I knew there was more than just the Socratic style of teaching and learning about the "real" world... Can you see where I am going with this?

To reinforce the science and especially applying my chemistry background, I read a supporting book called, <u>The Field: The Quest For The Secret Force Of The Universe</u>, by Lynne McTaggart. I highly recommend this book for anyone interested in understanding the science behind these concepts, even without a background in quantum physics.

The more I learned, the more I wanted to know. I started applying these concepts to events and people around me; judgmentally at first. In my newfound awareness, as many people do, I actually judged others by thinking things like,

> *"Well they are just not enlightened. I am more enlightened*
> *than they are. How sad for them. I think I could teach*
> *them to be more like me, if they would just see it my way.*
> *Maybe one day they will be as spiritual as I am."*

Now if that is not ego, I don't know what is. It is amazing how clever the ego is. I actually thought I was being more enlightened that someone else, or that my spirit was more spiritual than another. I was predominantly judging others on a competitive level of spirituality; something akin to spiritual football. This is something that we must all be aware of as we grow and move forward into a new global consciousness.

As I have grown and continue to grow, I have found that my true connection, my true self is humble. If we are not in service to others it is not spirit. If we are worried that someone is not as good as we are or that we are not as good as them in our love of spirit, God, Jesus, Allah, Ra it is not spirit.

> *If we wear our spirituality like a sheriffs*
> *badge, then it is NOT spirit. It is ego.*

Spirit is humble, joyful, caring, uplifting, and most importantly, our common source spirit is *love*. It can be found every day and in every way. We must seek deeper levels, and joyfully be accepting of others without judgments. Remember...

> *Judge not that ye be not judged*
> *Matthew 7:1*

Our presence in others lives should fill them with hope and bring calm to their being. This only comes without judging others and by loving unconditionally.

There are examples of spirit, even in television programs. Here is a portion of dialogue between Sam Malone and Norm Peterson in the last episode of a television sitcom called Cheers:

Norm: Sammy, I didn't want to say this in front of the others but you know what I think the most important thing in life is? It's love, and you want to know what I love?

> *Sam: Beer, Norm?*
> *Norm (checks his watch): Yeah I'll have a quick one....*
> *Later in dialogue*
> *Norm: I don't think it matters what you love Sammy. It could be a person. It could be a thing. As long as you love it completely and without judgment*

This came from a sitcom. But it really expresses in a short comic situation that Love is the answer. I am not talking about infatuation or lust.

I am describing the love of source. That common ground upon which we all have the same footing and that we all return. The illumination of the ego world for what it is.

We must function in this physical world and there will always be those that are still learning their lessons and may be mostly in the Ego "real" World, but if we can always return fear with love we can move all of existence to a new reality.

I believe that this is the hope for all spiritual leaders. It is the hope for this high school science teacher.

As I continue to learn and grow in the understanding of this common connection, I feel it growing in me on a daily basis. There were times when I felt overwhelmed by it. Now I am simply happy to be present in it, and happy to be a role model of it to the people, especially the young people that I come in contact with on a daily basis.

> *It takes courage... to endure the sharp pain of self-discovery rather than choose to take the dull pain of unconsciousness that would last the rest of our lives*
> *Mariannne Williamson, Return to Love*

I am a regular man, with regular struggles. I have emotional pain, and physical pain. I sometimes feel as though I am a victim, but soon realize the level of audacity that is, so I have learned to let that go.

I realize that I continue to grow on a daily basis and enjoy the journey. This is one of the reasons that I wrote this book.

I love to watch football and rooting for the Chicago Bears, but I also find myself in a conundrum about how to reconcile the shear egoic world of this activity with the sense of who I truly am. I think that this is a struggle that we all have to deal with in one form or another.

I have a T-shirt that has two sayings on it. The front says "More Cowbell" ascribed as a reminder of a humorous Saturday Night Live skit with Christopher Walken. On the back is one of my favorite spiritual sayings. "Treat All Life as Sacred." To me, this is the perfect metaphor for the manner in which I try to live. I live in the physical and sometimes egocentric world, but I approach my life and those around me in spirit and in love.

I do not know but it will be difficult at this point for everyone to make a uniform transition into total spiritual awareness in all situations, but I do think that we can strive to recognize the truth in us, and see it in others. In doing so we take a new step into a new collective consciousness. One in which we experience the joyful "real" world.

I think that the first step is important, and that is recognizing who you really are and how we are all woven together in a tapestry of universe.

It is not that the world is abundant… we are abundance.
We don't do service… we are service.
We don't get love… we are love

These realizations bring us all closer to the connection that we have to each other and to the Loving God-universe that we partake in. With this recognition, there is hope and through love we can all be a part of the journey together.

Namaste'

Afterword

It is my hope that this book can bring a smile to your face and joy in the recognition that we are not as different as was once believed. I look forward to feedback from anyone and everyone that reads this, and know that my intention is based solely out of love. Feel free to email me at coachsteg@me.com

Notes:

Credits and recommended reading

Books

* Beckwith, M.B, (2008). *Spiritual Liberation. Fulfilling Your Souls Potential.* New York: Beyond Words Publisher

* Beckwith, M.B. (2009). *The Answer is You.* Califonia: Hay House Publishers

* Canfield, J., Hansen, M.V., McNamara, H. (1999). *Chicken Soup for the Unsinkable Soul.* Florida: Health Communications Publisher

* Chopra, D. (1994). *The Seven Spiritual Laws of Success.* California: Amber-Allen Publisher

* Chopra, D., Mlodinow, L. (2011). *War of the Worldviews. Science Vs Spirituality.* New York: Harmony Books Publisher

* Dyer, W (2009). *Excuses Be Gone!* California: Hay House Publisher

* Dyer, W (2006). *Being in Balance. 9 Principles for Creating Habits to Match Your Desires.* California: Hay House Publisher

*Dyer, W. (2007). *Change Your Thoughts-Change Your Life. Living the Wisdom of the Tao.* California: Hay House Publisher

* Dyer, W. (2001). *There's a Spiritual Solution to Every Problem.* HarperCollins Publishers

* Dyer, W (2010). *The Power of Intention*. California: Hay House Publisher

* Dyer, W. (2001). *10 Secrets for Success and Inner Peace*. California: Hay House Publisher

* Dyer, W. (2010). *The Shift. Taking Your Life from Ambition to Meaning*. California: Hay House Publisher

* Epstein, D.M., (1994). *The 12 Stages of Healing. A Network Approach to Wholeness.I California: Amber-Allen Publisher*

* Edwards, L.C., (2005). *Spiritual Laws That Govern Humanity and the Universe*. California: Grand Lodge of the English language Jurisdiction, AMORC Publishers

* Fulghum, R. (1988). *All I really Need to Know I learned in Kindergarten*. New York: Random House Publisher

*Hawkins, D.R., (2002). *Power VS. Force. The Hidden determinants of Human Behavior*. California: Hay House Publisher

* Ferrini, P., (1994). *Love Without Conditions. Reflections of the Christ Mind*. Massachusetts: Heartways Press Publisher

* Jampolsky, G.G., (1979, 2004). *Love is Letting Go of Fear*. California: Celestial Arts Publisher

* Morter, T. M., (1997). *Dynamic Health: Using Your Own Beliefs, Thoughts and Memory to Create Healthy Body*. Arkansas: Best Research Publisher

* McTaggart, L. (2001). *The Field. The Quest for the Secret Force of the Universe*. Great Britain: Harper Collins Publishers

* Moore, T. (1994). *Soul Mates. Honoring the Mysteries of Love and Relationship*. New York: Harper Collins

* Moore, T., Thomas, P., (1994). *Care of the Soul: A Guide for Cultivating Depth and sacredness in Everyday Life.* New York: Harper Collins

* Rohr, R. (2003). *Everything Belongs.* New York: The Crossroad Publisher

* Ruiz, M. (1997). *The Four Agreements: A Practical Guide to Personal freedom.* California: Amber-Allen Publisher

* Stone, H., Stone, S., (1989). *Embracing Ourselves. The Voice dialogue Manual.* California: Nataraj Publisher

* Tolle, E., (1999). *The Power of Now. A Guide to Spiritual Enlightenment.* Canada: Namaste' Publisher

* Tolle, E, (2005). *A New Earth. Awakening to Your Life's Purpose.* New York: The Penguin Group Publisher

* Vanzant, I., (1998). *In the Meantime. Finding Yourself and the Love You Want.* New York: Fireside Publisher

* Wapnick, K., (1978). *Christian Psychology in a Course in Miracles.* New York: Foundation for a Course in Miracles Publisher

* Wapnick, K., (2005). *The healing Power of Kindness. Forgiving Our Limitations.* California: Foundation for a Course in Miracles Publisher

* Waters, O., (2006). *The Shift. The revolution in Human Consciousness.* Delaware: Infinite Being Publisher

* Sykes, C. J. (1995), *Dumbing Down Our Kids. Why America's Children Feel Good About Themselves but Can't Read, Write, or Add.* New York: St Martin's Press Publisher

* Conquest, R. (1990), *The Great Terror. 40th Anniversary Ed.*

New York: Oxford University Press Publisher

* Greene, B., (2003), *The Elegant Universe. Superstrings, Hidden Dimensions, and the Quest, for the Ultimate Theory*, United States: WW Norton and Company Inc Publisher

Webpages

* *Arendzen, J. (1909). Gnosticism. In <u>The Catholic Encyclopedia.</u> New York: Robert Appleton Company. Retrieved March 9, 2012 from New Advent: http://www.newadvent.org/cathen/06592a.htm*

*Gandhi, M., (2012) Quote DB, http://www.quotedb.com/quotes/2066

* Various Authors, *www.quotegarden.com/live-now.html* (2012)

* Various Authors, http://en.wikipedia.org/wiki/Main_Page

* Various Authors, (2012),http://life.gaiam.com/

* Author unknown, (2008) http://www.inspirationalstories.com/happiness-4.html

* Various Authors, (2011), http://www.humblelibertarian.com/2010/04/100-great-anti-war-quotes.html

* US Gov, (2009), http://nces.ed.gov/pubs2009/2009030.pdf

* Various Authors, (2012), *Online Christian Library*, http://biblos.com/

* Alexander, G, (2002), http://answers.google.com/answers/threadview?id=5096

* Various Authors, (2010), *Psychological Harassment Information Association.* http://www.psychologicalharassment.com/

psychological_manipulation.htm#Psychological_Warfare_
Bullies_Criminals

* Autheor Unknown, (2008-2012), *Our Stressful Lives*. *http://www.*
ourstressfullives.com/stress-statistics.html

* Schulz, M., Woolsey, B. (2012), *Credit Card Statistics, Industry*
Facts, Debt Statististics. http://www.creditcards.com/credit-card-
news/credit-card-industry-facts-personal-debt-statistics-1276.
php

* Sol, (2003), *The Seven Chokras and Their Meanings*. *http://www.*
mysticfamiliar.com/library/l_chakras.htm#third

* Vaious Authors, (1999-2012), *Urban Dictionary, http://www.*
urbandictionary.com/

* United States Government (NOAA), (2012), *State of Climate*.
http://www.ncdc.noaa.gov/sotc/

* Smith, N. (2004), *Whole Systems Foundation*. http://www.whole-
systems.org/home.html

Video Citations
* Chasse, B., Arntz, W., Vicente, M (producers), Chasse, B., Arntz,
W. (directors) (2004), *What the Bleep do we Know?* United
States: Capri Films

* Bender, L. Burns, S., David, L. (Producer), Guggenheim, D.
(Director, (2006), *An Inconvenient Truth*, United States:
Paramount Classics

* Harrington, P. (Producer), Heriot, D.(Director), (2006), *The*
Secret, Australia: Prime Time Productions